The Cheese Biscuit Queen Tells All

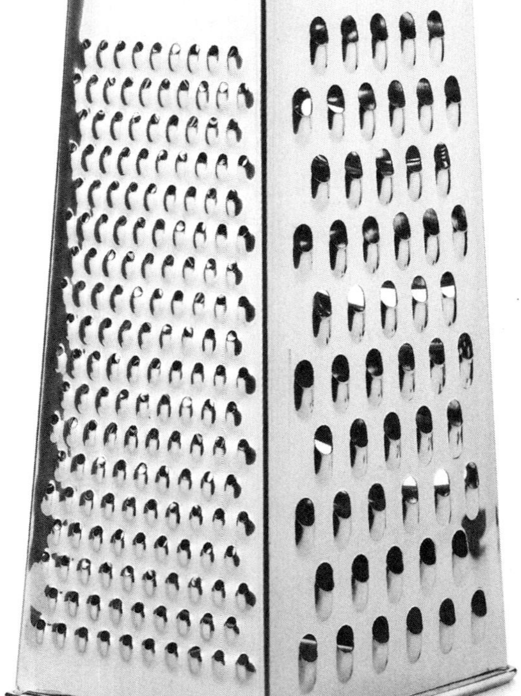

The Cheese Biscuit Queen Tells All

Southern Recipes,
Sweet Remembrances,
and a Little Rambunctious Behavior

Mary Martha Greene

THE UNIVERSITY OF
SOUTH CAROLINA PRESS

Published by the University of South Carolina Press
Columbia, South Carolina 29208

www.uscpress.com

Photo credits—istockphoto.com: grater, karandaev; tiara, SergValen; timer, alicjane; butter, Tomas_Mina; silver utensils, Martina_L; china plate, KarpenkovDenis; wood spoons, Santje09; glass bowl, urfinguss; brown egg, kool99; measuring spoons images, marekuliasz; peeler, gresei; metal measuring cup, sarahdoow; meat thermometer, NorGal; skillet, StephanieFrey; meat fork, Yevhenii Orlov; lemon, Kelenart; ladel, vikif; offset spatula, tapui; beaters, Giambra; whisk, chengyuzheng; peg measurer, ahirao_photo.

Manufactured in the United States of America

30 29 28 27 26 25 24 23 22 21
10 9 8 7 6 5 4 3

Library of Congress Cataloging-in-Publication Data
can be found at http://catalog.loc.gov/.

ISBN 978-1-64336-182-6 (paperback)
ISBN 978-1-64336-183-3 (ebook)

To all my mothers . . . Gran-Gran, Mother, Mary Dob, Mimi, Dessie, and Miss Kitty . . . great cooks and even better women. I am forever grateful for your bountiful love and nurturing.

Contents

Introduction

"A shared recipe in the South is more precious than gold . . .
and it always comes with a good story."

—As seen on a tea towel

At the funeral of my dear friend Shirley Mills' mother, Queen Isabella Mills, the minister quoted an African proverb: "As long as your story is being told, you never really die." I would amend that to read, "As long as your story is being told, and your recipes are being passed down, you never really die."

And so it began with this cookbook. As one of my goddaughters was leaving for a college semester at sea, she asked if I would teach her how to cook upon her return. I told her I'd do her one better: while she was gone, I'd write a cookbook of all my favorite recipes and those of my family, her family, and many others, with all the instructions she—and any other home cook—would need to recreate them as if I was in the kitchen at her side.

I want this cookbook to make you feel as if you are sitting down at the kitchen table with an old friend or family member, trading recipes and sharing stories. I am sure most cultures pass down their recipes, but I think Southerners are particularly fond of the practice. Many years of cooking with the fresh fruits and vegetables that grow plentifully in our climate, as well as the bountiful seafood available on our shores, have led to perfecting some pretty fine recipes for home dining.

I began looking for the family recipes that I'd put in a box when I inherited my grandmother's house in Beaufort and began renovating the kitchen. The box I'd thought they were in contained old tax returns, and I remembered that I'd taken a box of what I thought were tax returns to the accountant to be shredded. I was horrified at the thought that I'd shredded all my family recipes by mistake—and that they were gone forever.

One afternoon around the time my goddaughter was due back from her trip, I was cleaning out the pantry underneath the stairs and spotted the red top of my mother's recipe box in a big plastic storage tub. They are all there—my Mother's recipe box, my Aunt Mimi's, handwritten cards in my grandmother's handwriting that I haven't seen in years. Stained with vanilla or other remnants of long-ago family meals, they were restored to me. I spent the afternoon going through the box, tasting again, at least in my mind, all the dishes they made with love for so many years. After I posted a picture of the contents of the tub on social media, many friends who remembered the wonderful dishes my family prepared asked if I'd share the recipes. With that, the book I'd envisioned writing for my godchildren and next generation of cousins took on a greater audience.

As I wrote down the recipes, the stories naturally started flowing along with them. I hope you'll enjoy the stories as much as the recipes. Some of the names and details have been changed to protect the guilty parties (and you know who you are), but the essence remains the same. These stories represent so many happy dinners, holiday meals, and special occasions celebrated with family and friends. I've used cooking and baking to win friends and influence people both in my lobbying career and when entertaining business prospects for clients, and many of these stories came from those events. Great food leads to great times and great memories, making everyday meals feel like special, memorable occasions.

Several of the stories involve the death or funeral of a loved one. Food is such an essential part of any Southern funeral. I believe it's also part of the healing process. Shortly after my brother died, the son of dear friends of mine underwent a major surgery. By taking dinner over to them, I felt as if my healing process had begun, and I was moving forward. Someone other than me needed to be nurtured by food, so the focus was shifting from my grief to helping others. This is yet another sign of the healing power of food.

I bake every week with some wonderful young people at a drop-in center for at-risk youth. The first time we baked together, I was struck by the happy memories they associated with food. Many of these youth were homeless or had other at-risk living situations, but almost all of them had a happy food memory. They told me, "I cooked that with my grandmother," or, "My mother used to make these for us." This reminded me that food elicits powerful memories.

Food reminds us who we are and where we came from. Once, while I was making my mother's grasshopper pie for Easter, I chatted with my friend, the author Bren McClain. I told Bren that I wasn't sure whether my craving was for the pie or for the happy memories of my family that went along with it. It might have been a little of both.

I am very fortunate to have grown up in the kitchen with many wonderful cooks. My mother, who was a home economics major in college, was a very exacting cook, baker, and meal planner. My grandmother was a wonderful country cook who made the best creamed corn God ever put on this green Earth. My Aunt Mary wasn't much of a cook, but she could make the best fried chicken and milk gravy. After she retired, she learned to make sourdough bread. (Sadly, I don't think she ever wrote either of the recipes down, as I could find no trace of them.) And my Aunt Mimi was the Cheese Biscuit Queen of the world—and had many other fabulous recipes as well.

Dessie, the wonderful woman who helped rear my brother George and me, was another very important influence on my life and cooking skills. She also taught me the important lesson that you do *not* go into someone else's pot without their permission. (A high school friend of my brother's learned this the hard way when he opened one of Dessie's pots and was swiftly met by a wooden spoon across the back of his hand!)

I like to think of my cooking as a combination of the culinary talents of all these influential women.

I have always loved cookbooks, going back to when I was in third grade and bought my first very own cookbook—the 1965 edition of the *Betty Crocker Boys and Girls Cookbook* with the yellow striped cover. (Betty was pretty progressive for the time, expecting boys to learn how to cook, but I do think it should have been the *Girls and Boys Cookbook*! Although my dad and brother always cooked, that definitely wasn't the norm in the 1960s.) Betty's cookbook inspired both my lifelong love of cookbooks and the joy of reading a cookbook and imagining what a dish would taste like. My aunt Lou (see stories and recipes for her Chocolate Roll and Shrimp Curry, pages 208 and 136) was the first person I ever heard talk about reading a cookbook like you would a novel and enjoying and savoring all the wisdom contained within the pages.

I hope these stories will make you laugh and maybe cry a little, and that they will elicit some happy memories of your own. It is my wish that you'll enjoy the recipes and use them to create some food memories with your friends and family. And, for goodness' sake, write down your recipes so you can pass them along to future generations!

Mary Martha Greene

Aunt Mimi's Famous Cheese Biscuits

This recipe is in a league all by itself. The basic recipe can be found in numerous cookbooks from the 1950s, but I think Aunt Mimi, my mother's youngest sister, made so many of them over the next sixty years that she perfected them. She was known throughout South Carolina and beyond for her cheese biscuits. When my pregnant friends experienced morning sickness, my Aunt Mimi's cheese biscuits rushed to the rescue. (I thought the son of one of my friends might be born with pockmarks because of the Rice Krispies in all the cheese biscuits his mother had eaten while she was expecting him.) When my brother George and other friends were going through chemotherapy, those cheese biscuits came to the rescue again.

Once, many years ago, I had to be in Washington, DC, for a lobbying trip at the same time my mother and Aunt Mimi had to come to Columbia for a luncheon and portrait dedication at the State House. They were going to spend the night at my house, and I asked my best friend Jane if she would bring my four-year-old goddaughter Windy to visit them after preschool.

Windy's preschool was only a few blocks from my house, and all the way there, Jane reiterated to Windy that she was not to ask for any cheese biscuits. If "Miss Mimi" offered her some, she could have them, but she was not to ask. They got to the house and Mother, Mimi, and Jane began visiting and chatting. No mention was made of cheese biscuits.

After a while, Windy sidled up to the chair Mimi was sitting in, lowered her head, looked up at Mimi with her big blue eyes, and said, just as pitifully as she could possibly muster, "We don't have any cheese biscuits at *our* house." Well, of course Mimi jumped up when she realized they didn't have any cheese biscuits. They all went in the kitchen and pulled out all the accoutrements of a proper cheese biscuit tea party. (Now in Windy's defense, Mimi almost always brought her some cheese biscuits when they came to visit. Jane said she couldn't punish Windy because, in fact, she had not asked for any cheese biscuits.) For the rest of Aunt Mimi's life, we used "we don't have any cheese biscuits at *our* house" as our way of scheming to get cheese biscuits. And when that beautiful little blue-eyed girl grew up and got married, plenty of cheese biscuits were served at the reception.

Mimi, who loved to travel, grew up in the generation where you always brought something to share with your fellow travelers on the tour bus. Her cheese biscuits have gone with us to Ireland, Alaska, and China, so they've literally traveled the world.

Mimi's biscuits were featured in an article in *The State* newspaper on the condition that they wouldn't print the calorie count—that would have taken all the joy out of them! I told Allison Askins, the food editor at the time, "You could write a whole article on those cheese biscuits—countries they have visited . . . and the lies, half-truths, cheating, and conniving small children (not to mention grown adults) have done to get them." During a phone interview, the ever-gracious Mimi told Allison, "Those cheese biscuits have gone all up and down the East Coast—Washington, DC, Connecticut, and all around . . . I always laugh and say all obligations can be paid with cheese biscuits!"

I like to think that continuing to make these biscuits and sharing Aunt Mimi's recipe keeps her love and her legacy alive. I always have plates full of them scattered around my house for cocktail parties, and there are rarely any leftovers!

Mimi made her biscuits using an old-fashioned twelve-speed Sunbeam mixer with double beaters. If you have a modern stand mixer, I recommend using the whisk attachment to try to beat as much air into them as possible.

Makes 10 to 12 dozen

- 4 sticks Land O' Lakes margarine, at room temperature (see notes)
- 4 cups (1 pound) freshly grated Kraft extra-sharp Cheddar (see notes)
- ½ teaspoon ground cayenne pepper
- ¼ teaspoon smoked paprika (optional)
- 4½ cups sifted all-purpose flour (see notes)
- 4 cups Rice Krispies cereal

Preheat the oven to 350°F. Set aside 3 ungreased baking sheets.

Let the margarine and cheese come to room temperature, about 1 hour. (You can also warm both in the microwave for 20 seconds on high—you want them to soften, not melt.)

Using a stand mixer on medium-high speed, cream the margarine. Place half the cheese in the bowl of a food processor and process until it forms a ball or cream it by hand. Add the ball of cheese to the margarine and blend until the mixture is fully combined and creamy. Repeat with the other half of the cheese. Cream together the margarine and cheese until the mixture is smooth, has a light orange color, and resembles fluffy buttercream frosting. Add the ground cayenne pepper and the paprika, if using.

As the mixer continues to run on medium speed, gradually add the flour (see notes), ½ cup at a time, to the cheese mixture. After you have added 4½ cups of the sifted flour, return any additional flour to the bag for the next batch.

Place the Rice Krispies in a strainer with medium-to-large holes, if you have one, and shake any small pieces of cereal and sugar out of them. With the mixer running on low, gradually add the Rice Krispies to the mixture, 1 cup at a time.

Drop the batter by rounded teaspoons or balls from a #70 scoop onto the baking sheets. Press down lightly on the balls, making them about ¼-inch thick. Bake until lightly golden brown on the bottom, about 20 minutes. (Mimi would bake for 10 minutes and then switch the baking sheets between the top and bottom racks so that they would brown evenly on the top and the bottom.) Remove from the oven. If you have a partial sheet of biscuits, they will not require as much baking time, so adjust as necessary, probably around 15 to 16 minutes.

As soon as they come out of the oven, transfer the biscuits to paper towels spread on a clean countertop to absorb the grease. Set aside to cool for 10 to 15 minutes. As soon as they have cooled, serve or transfer the biscuits to airtight containers so they do not reabsorb any grease. Biscuits will keep in a tin on the counter for up to a week or can be frozen in the airtight containers for up to two months. Mimi used to reheat them for a few minutes on a baking sheet in a warm oven to "freshen" them up, and then act like she'd just baked them when anyone dropped by to visit.

NOTES: Use Land O'Lakes and Kraft brands for best results. While Mimi always used margarine in her cheese biscuits, I now use 2 sticks of butter and 2 sticks of margarine. I find that using only butter makes them too greasy and not light and fluffy, like Aunt Mimi's biscuits. It also makes them spread out too much.

Do not use pregrated cheese; it contains a wax coating that will ruin the consistency of the biscuits.

Using a large, slotted spoon, fluff the flour in the bag before measuring it out. Sift it and then remeasure the flour.

A Little Queenly Insight

A big part of baking, in addition to using the best possible ingredients, is making sure you have the right tools and bakeware. It will probably come as no surprise that I collect various baking pans. I think of bakeware like little children think of toys—it's what I like to play with. Craft stores usually have a good selection of pans, and you can quickly grow your collection using the discount coupons they offer online or in the newspaper.

I recommend:

- Two 9 × 5-inch pans
- Two medium muffin tins with 12 (2½-inch) wells each
- Three miniature muffin tins with 12 (1¾-inch) wells each
- One 9 × 13-inch pan
- Three 9- or 10-inch round cake pans
- One 10-inch tube pan for pound cakes (this is different from a Bundt pan)
- Three or more large baking sheets
- One jelly roll pan, which is really a baking sheet with ½-inch sides

Beyond these basics, you can expand your collection to fit however much storage space your kitchen will accommodate. I still have my mother's brioche molds, which I use every year to bake financiers, a type of dome-shaped French pastry, for a friend's birthday using a recipe from our favorite bakery in Maine.

I also love to bake individual pound cakes in 2 × 4-inch brownie pans; I store the cakes in the freezer so I have dessert ever at the ready. These pans have multiple wells in them, like muffin tins, but the wells are rectangular in shape. I also have a variety of springform pans ranging from 4 to 9 inches to bake both sweet and savory cheesecakes. And in my kitchen, the 5 × 16-inch loaf pan that my best friend's mother Kitty Windham always baked her pound cake in is a must!

One of my favorite pieces of bakeware is the miniature muffin tin. I like the old-fashioned twelve-cup tins that are made of aluminum. As a matter of fact, I don't just like them—I hoard them. For a while, when any of my friends who were downsizing their parents' homes would ask, "Is there anything out of the house you'd like?" I'd respond, without missing a beat, "miniature muffin tins!" When I last counted, I had more than twenty-five of them. I find that they just bake better than the new nonstick ones—spray those babies up and have at it. They're just right for creating bite-size treats—whether they're sweet or savory!

A key baking technique is using a lever scoop to make sure your muffins, cookies, and cupcakes are of a uniform size . . . not to mention how much time it saves versus dropping each using a spoon or measuring out portion sizes. I don't think I could cook or bake without them. They're especially handy for the cheese biscuits I make by the thousands at Christmastime, as they make the process go so much faster. I use them for apportioning crab cakes and fillings for oyster pastries, and they can also be used as melon ballers.

The scoop size, which equals the number of portions of that size per quart of food, is usually specified on the lever that rotates to extract the food or the scoop's packaging. If you are not sure about your scoop's capacity, get out your measuring cups and spoons and measure them using water.

SCOOP #	SCOOP VOLUME	DIAMETER	USE FOR
#12	⅓ cup	2½ inches	Crab cakes
#16	¼ cup	2⅜ inches	Large muffins
#24	8 teaspoons	1⅞ inches	Medium muffins
#50	2 tablespoons	1½ inches	Large drop cookies Mini muffins
#70	2 teaspoons	1⅜ inches	Medium drop cookies Mini crab cakes Cheese biscuits
#100	1½ teaspoons	1¼ inches	Small drop cookies Fillings for grits and red rice tarts
#110	1 teaspoon	1 inch	Benne seed wafers

And, of course, you can use them for their old-fashioned purpose: plopping ice cream on top of pecan tarts or apple pie!

1

Breakfast Baking

All Hail the Queen

It was a long-standing joke in my family that Aunt Mimi, my mother's youngest sister, looked like Queen Elizabeth II. Even at an early age, she strongly resembled the queen. She loved to wear hats, wore gloves long after most ladies abandoned them, and had a pocketbook for every occasion—all adding to her queen-like persona. Mimi, however, failed to see the resemblance; or, if she did, she just wouldn't admit it.

In the fall of 2002, for her 80th birthday, Mimi and I took a trip to Alaska, and along the way, we stopped in Victoria, British Columbia. Mimi wanted to stay overnight and have tea at the Empress Hotel, where she and my mother had visited many years earlier. On our first night in Victoria, as we walked to dinner along the inner harbor, a street performer in full Elizabethan costume rushed up to Aunt Mimi and bowed before her, à la Sir Walter Raleigh, exalting, "My queen, my queen." Well, Mimi thought we were about to get mugged and clutched her pocketbook even tighter than before. The next day, in one of the shops that sold heraldry china associated with the royal family, an older lady about Mimi's age also commented on her resemblance to QE II. Once again, Queen Mimi was not amused.

Aunt Mimi (right) looking very queenly, ready for my cousin Patty's wedding in January 1968.

Several years later, shortly after the real Queen Elizabeth and Prince Philip visited President and Mrs. George W. Bush in the White House, Mimi and my mother stopped by the post office in Beaufort. The young lady working behind the counter looked at Aunt Mimi and said in her best Lowcountry accent, "You know, you kinda favah' the Queen!"

With that, Aunt Mimi kind of had to admit that she "favored" Queen Elizabeth. After all, Mimi was the Cheese Biscuit Queen of Beaufort, so there you have it. All hail the Queen!

Country Ham Scones with Fig Butter

If you can't make it to the Empress Hotel for tea, bring a little English style to your own breakfast table and try these scones. These scones have always been a favorite in my family, especially with the Queen.

Makes 16 scones

COUNTRY HAM SCONES

1¾ cups all-purpose flour

¼ cup hush puppy mix with onion (I prefer House Autry brand for this recipe)

2 tablespoons granulated sugar

2 teaspoons baking powder

½ teaspoon salt

¼ teaspoon ground cayenne pepper

6 tablespoons cold unsalted butter

1 cup slivered cooked country ham

1 cup buttermilk or whole milk

FIG BUTTER

2 tablespoons fig preserves

8 tablespoons unsalted butter (1 stick), softened

Pinch of ground cinnamon

Preheat the oven to 425°F. Lightly grease a baking sheet and set aside.

Make the Country Ham Scones: Combine the flour, hush puppy mix, sugar, baking powder, salt, and cayenne pepper in a bowl. Cut the butter into small pieces and, using a pastry blender or fork, blend them into the bowl until the mixture is crumbly. Stir in the ham. Using a spoon, stir in the buttermilk just until the dry ingredients are moistened.

Turn out the dough on a lightly floured surface and knead 3 to 4 times (the dough should remain moist). Divide the dough in half. Pat each half into a circle and transfer to the prepared baking sheet. Using a knife, score each half into 8 wedges, but do not cut all the way through the dough or separate the wedges. (If you wish to make smaller tea scones, divide the dough into thirds and then score them.)

Bake until the scones are light golden brown, 24 to 26 minutes. Remove from the oven and set aside to cool slightly.

Make the Fig Butter: If the fig preserves contain whole figs or are very chunky, mash them well with a fork.

Using a hand mixer or stand mixer on medium speed, cream the butter until fluffy. Add the fig preserves and cinnamon and mix until well blended.

Using a knife, separate the cooled wedges and serve with the room-temperature Fig Butter.

NOTE: These are great to take along on a weekend trip if you want to make something special for breakfast. First, combine all the dry ingredients, cut in the butter, and transfer the mixture to a ziplock bag or other container. Chop the ham and place it in a separate bag; measure out the buttermilk into a glass jar; and throw everything in a cooler. When you are ready to make breakfast, simply mix together the ingredients and bake. You'll always be invited back!

Felix's Sunday Morning French Toast

When I was a little girl, mornings were a chance to have some one-on-one time with my father. My mother was usually getting ready to go teach school, and my older brother liked to sleep late, so mornings at the breakfast table were our time together. I'm sure he would have preferred to enjoy a second cup of coffee and read his newspaper in peace, but he always made time for me.

Most weekday mornings, he'd cook bacon, eggs, and grits for my mother and himself and leave the rest on the stove for Dessie, George, and me. He'd also make their coffee in a percolator. I always loved waking up to the smell of coffee and the gurgling sound of the coffee being sucked up through the filter and then dripping back down into the pot.

My mother and grandmother used to make something they called "master mix" long before Bisquick came along. It was a kind of baking mix you could use to make biscuits, waffles, or pancakes. On Saturdays, Daddy would make either waffles or pancakes using the master mix, but Sunday mornings were reserved for his French toast (I guess it was quick and easy when we were trying to get out the door to church). His recipe was taped on the inside of one of the kitchen cabinets. It was written in the distinctive handwriting he learned from my grandfather, who was an electrical

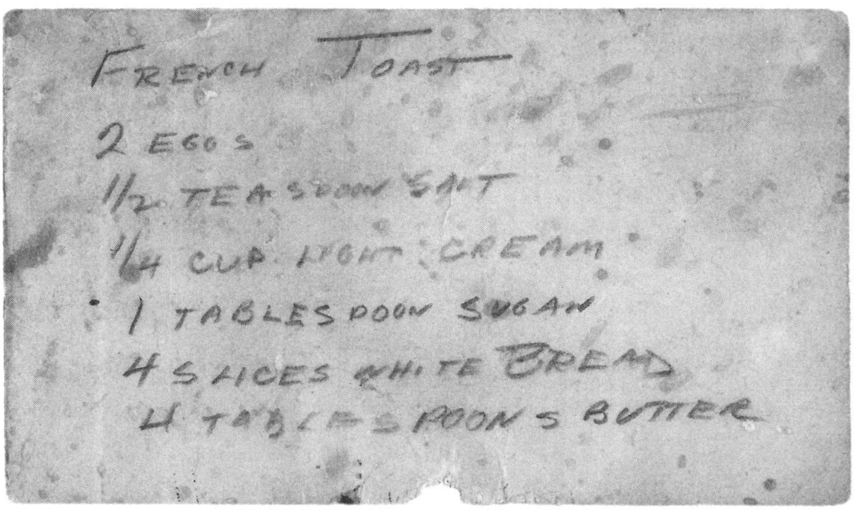

FRENCH TOAST

2 EGGS

1/2 TEASPOON SALT

1/4 CUP LIGHT CREAM

1 TABLESPOON SUGAR

4 SLICES WHITE BREAD

4 TABLESPOONS BUTTER

Daddy's French toast recipe in his distinctive handwriting.

contractor—all capitals, even the lowercase letters. I still have it framed in my kitchen today. Daddy always used basic Sunbeam white sandwich bread, but I use good-quality brioche, challah, or sourdough bread.

In Daddy's last year, when he was recovering from a stroke, he had me take him to Kmart to buy a wheeled cart. He would hang on and push it around the kitchen, transporting ingredients from the refrigerator to the stove, so he could continue to cook breakfast for my mother before she went to school each morning. Daddy died during my senior year of college, and I have missed him every day since.

Makes 2 servings

2 whole large eggs

¼ cup whole milk

1 tablespoon granulated sugar

½ teaspoon vanilla extract

½ teaspoon salt

4 tablespoons unsalted butter

4 slices bread

Warmed syrup, ground cinnamon, confectioners' sugar, and fruit for serving

Whisk the eggs in a large, flat bowl. Add the milk and whisk to combine. Stir in the sugar, vanilla, and salt.

Melt the butter on a griddle or in a large frying pan. Dip both sides of each piece of bread into the egg mixture and transfer to the hot griddle. Cook until golden brown, and then flip over and cook on the other side until golden brown. Remove from the heat.

Serve with the warmed syrup, cinnamon, confectioners' sugar, and fruit. I top French toast with sliced strawberries or peaches when they are in season.

Apple Toffee Muffins

From the time I was a child, fall meant a trip to the North Carolina mountains. Blowing Rock, Boone, Asheville, Hendersonville, and Flat Rock were family favorites. As an adult, I also came to love Highlands and Cashiers. My mother's family were from the foothills of South Carolina, and as much as she came to love the Lowcountry, she couldn't wait to get a first glimpse of the mountains whenever we headed that way. A stop for apples was always on the agenda for the trip—we loved the ones from Sky Top and Edneyville.

After we returned with apples from any fall trip, these muffins soon followed. The recipe is adapted from one from the beautiful Cuthbert House Inn in Beaufort. They're always a popular treat—not just in the fall, but any time of year. They freeze very well and can easily be reheated by wrapping them in foil and placing them in a warm oven.

Makes 24 muffins

1 cup buttermilk

1 teaspoon baking soda

1 whole large egg

1½ cups packed light brown sugar

⅔ cup vegetable oil

1 teaspoon ground cinnamon

1 teaspoon salt

1 teaspoon vanilla extract

2½ cups all-purpose flour

1½ cups diced Granny Smith apples

1 cup chopped pecans or walnuts

1 cup Bits O'Brickle English Toffee Bits

¼ cup granulated sugar

Preheat the oven to 325°F. Grease two ½-cup muffin tins (each with 12 wells) with butter or baking spray with flour and set aside.

Combine the buttermilk and baking soda in a small bowl or measuring cup and stir until the baking soda is dissolved.

Beat the egg in a large bowl. Add the brown sugar and oil and whisk together. Add the cinnamon, salt, and vanilla and stir well. Add the flour, about ½ cup at a time, and the buttermilk mixture, about ¼ a cup at a time, beginning and ending with flour. Mix well after each addition until all the flour is incorporated. Add the apples, nuts, and toffee bits to the batter.

Scoop the batter into the muffin tins using a large serving spoon or a #16 scoop. Sprinkle the granulated sugar over the top of each muffin.

Bake for 30 minutes. Remove from the oven and set aside to cool for about 5 minutes.

Transfer the muffins from the pan to a wire rack to finish cooling. Serve warm.

Homemade Apple Fritters

My friend Lester Laminack, a noted children's author and educator, wrote a wonderful book called *Saturdays and Teacakes* about baking with his grandmother when he was a little boy. Lester sent me this recipe for apple fritters, and I promised to make it for him when we all were together again in Beaufort. That day finally came one cold February afternoon, and, joined by our friends Sandy and Sally Somerall, we instituted the Fridays and Fritters Club. These are easy to make and so much better when they are served warm! To make peach fritters, substitute 1 cup chopped peaches for the apple.

Makes 8 to 10 fritters

FRITTERS

1 cup all-purpose flour

2 tablespoons packed light brown sugar

1½ teaspoons baking powder

1 teaspoon ground cinnamon

1 teaspoon salt

2 whole large eggs, beaten

⅓ cup whole milk

1 tablespoon unsalted butter, melted

1 cup chopped apple (any type)

Canola or vegetable oil for frying

GLAZE

2 cups confectioners' sugar

6 tablespoons whole milk

Make the Fritters: Combine the flour, brown sugar, baking powder, cinnamon, and salt in a medium bowl. Stir in the eggs, milk, and butter until just combined. Fold in the apple.

In a frying pan over medium-high heat, pour enough oil to come about halfway up the side of the pan and heat the oil to 350°F. Test the oil by throwing a small amount of batter into it—if it floats to the top, it's ready. (Do not overheat the oil; it will cause the outside of the fritter to burn before the insides have fully cooked.) Carefully add the batter to the oil in using a ¼ cup measure. Cook each fritter until brown, about 2 minutes, and then flip, pressing slightly to flatten the fritter. Cook another 1 to 2 minutes, until both sides are browned. Transfer the fritters briefly to a plate lined with paper towels to absorb any excess oil and then transfer to a wire rack to cool to the touch.

Make the Glaze: Stir the confectioners' sugar and milk together in a small bowl.

Dunk the top of each fritter into the glaze. Place on a rack for 3 minutes to allow the glaze to harden and then dunk the other side. Best served warm.

Maine Blueberry Streusel Muffins

We've been fortunate enough to be invited to spend time at a friend's family home in beautiful Blue Hill, Maine, on several occasions. Each time we visit, we take some time to make these wonderful muffins for breakfast and share them with our hosts. Our friend's father once said, "They always feed me so good when they come to visit."

I love using fresh, tiny Maine blueberries to make them—once, I even toted some home in my carry-on bag to make these muffins for friends back in Beaufort. As I was going through security, my bag was snatched off the conveyor belt, and the TSA agent loudly proclaimed, "Whose bag is *this?*"

I always try to be careful with what I put in my carry-on bag, so I identified myself and stepped over to the table of shame where they had moved my bag. As the agent started unpacking it, he announced—again, very loudly—that it had tested positive for *explosives!* Now, other than lighting up an occasional sparkler in the back yard, I am typically not an explosives kind of girl, so I couldn't imagine what was testing positive among the contents. The TSA agent zeroed in on the tin that contained the blueberries.

"What's this?" he asked accusingly. The berries were in a Christmas tin, so I wondered if one of my friend's children had handled it on Christmas Eve after shooting off some fireworks. I was in the middle of explaining this as he pried off the lid to reveal my big crime. Instead, he revealed fresh Maine produce to everyone within blueberry-rolling distance.

Tiny little blueberries spilled all over the Portland airport—the table, my suitcase, him, me—you get the picture.

"You didn't tell me there were blueberries in here," he says.

"You didn't ask!" I replied.

He then explained that blueberries apparently possess some of the same qualities as explosives. After swabbing the top of the tin, he returned it and the remaining blueberries and sent me on my way. So when you're going through security at the Portland airport, be careful not to step on the rest of them, as they went all over God's creation. I'm sure they're still trying to track them all down.

If fresh Maine blueberries aren't available, you can use frozen ones. Allow the berries to thaw and then rinse them and spread them on paper towels to dry. To prevent the berries from discoloring the batter, stir them with 1 tablespoon of flour until well coated before adding the batter.

Makes 24 muffins

MUFFINS

1½ cups fresh or frozen blueberries

⅓ cup granulated sugar

4 tablespoons (½ stick) unsalted butter, softened

1 whole large egg

2½ cups all-purpose flour

1 tablespoon + 2 teaspoons baking powder

½ teaspoon salt

1 cup whole milk

1 teaspoon vanilla extract

STREUSEL TOPPING

½ cup granulated sugar

½ cup all-purpose flour

½ teaspoon ground cinnamon

4 tablespoons (½ stick) unsalted butter, softened

Make the Muffins: Preheat the oven to 375°F. Grease two ½-cup muffin tins (each with 12 wells) with butter or baking spray with flour and set aside.

If using fresh blueberries, pick through the berries to make sure all stems are removed. Rinse in a colander and spread them out on paper towels to dry.

Using a hand mixer or a stand mixer on medium-high speed, cream together the sugar and butter. Add the egg and beat until the mixture is light and fluffy.

In a separate bowl, sift together the flour, baking powder, and salt. Reduce the mixer speed to medium low, and as the mixer continues to run, gradually add the dry ingredient mixture to the sugar mixture, alternating it with the milk. Add the vanilla and stir until well blended. Using a spatula, gently stir in the blueberries, taking care to not break or crush them.

Make the Streusel: Combine the dry ingredients in a small bowl. Using a fork, cut the butter into the flour mixture until it resembles crumbs.

Spoon the batter into the prepared muffin tins (a #16 scoop works well for filling large muffin tins). Sprinkle 1 teaspoon of the streusel topping over each muffin and press down lightly with the back of a spoon to help the topping stick to the muffins. Bake until the tops are lightly browned, 25 to 30 minutes. Remove from the oven and set on a wire rack to cool before serving.

Overnight Waffles

When my goddaughter Sally was little, she wasn't ever really bad; she was just always very *busy.* Whenever her mother Jane needed to let Sally know that she was serious, she'd bend over, gently put Sally's face in her hand, and pull it even with her face as she spoke to her.

Each day when Jane would arrive at preschool to pick her up, Sally would usually nod her head at her mother, suggesting, "Yes, I see that you are over there, but I'm going to finish up what I'm doing over here at this activity center." As Sally finished her business, Jane would talk with the teacher, asking how Sally had been that day, whether she had taken a nap, and so on—typical questions asked by the mother of a three-year-old.

One day, Jane arrived at the door, and *boom,* Sally was immediately at Jane's feet. "I want to hold you," Sally said, which was her version of, "I want you to pick me up." She'd hold up her arms and twinkle her fingers—you really couldn't resist her. But on this day, as Jane picked her up, Sally took Jane's face in her hand and pulled it even with her own little face.

"I be sweet tomorrow, Mommy," was all Sally said—her toddler way of saying, "If you could just spot me today and not ask the teacher about my day, I promise I'll do better tomorrow." Jane didn't ask, and we've always wondered what exactly Sally did that day that she needed to cover up. On many occasions since then, we've said "I be sweet tomorrow" to signal that we've had a really bad day.

These waffles are perfect for company breakfasts and weekend mornings. Mix most of it up the night before, and it'll sit there on the counter ready to *be sweet tomorrow.* Topped with warmed syrup and fresh fruit, it's an even more special treat.

Makes 8 to 10 waffles, depending on the size of your waffle iron

1 (¾-ounce) package active dry yeast

½ cup warm (105°F to 110°F) water

2 cups all-purpose flour

2 cups warm whole milk

8 tablespoons (1 stick) unsalted butter, melted

1 teaspoon granulated sugar

1 teaspoon vanilla extract

1 teaspoon salt

2 whole large eggs, beaten

¼ teaspoon baking soda

In a glass measuring cup, dissolve the yeast in the warm water. Set aside for 5 minutes.

Mix the flour, milk, butter, sugar, vanilla, and salt in a large mixing bowl. Add the yeast mixture and whisk well until the mixture is fully combined and has no lumps. Cover the bowl with plastic wrap and set aside at room temperature to rise overnight.

When ready to bake, stir the eggs and baking soda into the batter until well combined. Heat the waffle iron until the light indicates it is ready. Grease the waffle iron with baking spray with flour. Using a measuring cup, pour ¾ to 1 cup into the waffle iron, depending on capacity. Bake until the waffles are crispy and golden brown, 4 to 6 minutes. Remove from the waffle iron and serve; any leftover batter can be stored in the refrigerator for several days and baked later.

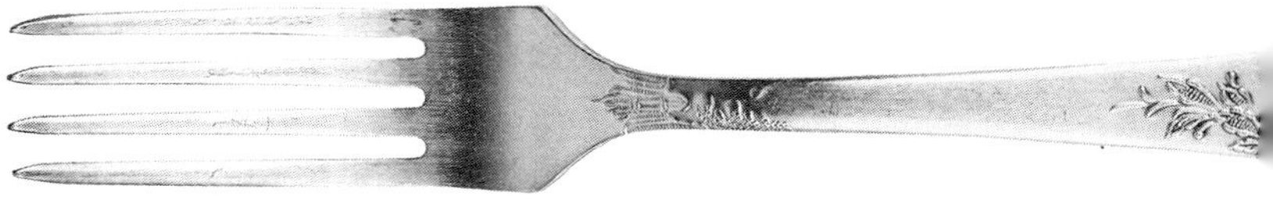

Miniature Sausage Muffins

These muffins are easy to make and very tasty. They are perfect for tailgating before early kickoff football games or as a hostess gift for a weekend invitation, and they're easy to freeze if you need to provide food for someone in need of care. I always tried to keep some in the freezer for my mother and aunts to enjoy for breakfast or with a bowl of soup for lunch. Since sausage typically comes in a 1-pound package, you may want to double the recipe and store extras in the freezer.

Makes 36 miniature muffins

- ½ pound bulk pork sausage
- ⅓ cup chopped green onions
- 1 (7½-ounce) package cheese- and garlic-flavored Bisquick biscuit mix or 1¾ cups Bisquick baking mix
- ½ cup finely grated Cheddar
- ½ teaspoon dry mustard
- ½ teaspoon garlic powder
- ¼ teaspoon ground cayenne pepper
- ½ cup whole milk or buttermilk

Preheat the oven to 400°F. Grease 3 miniature muffin tins, each with 12 (1¾-inch) wells, with baking spray with flour.

Combine the sausage and green onions in a skillet over medium heat and cook, breaking it apart with a spatula into crumbles, until the sausage is browned. Remove from the heat and transfer the sausage to a plate lined with paper towels to drain. Set aside to cool slightly.

Combine the biscuit mix, cheese, dry mustard, garlic powder, and cayenne pepper in a large bowl. Stir the drained sausage into the dry mixture. Add the milk, stirring just until moistened (the mixture will be thick).

Spoon or scoop the batter into the prepared muffin tins using a #50 scoop, filling each well two-thirds full. Bake until the muffins are golden brown, 14 to 16 minutes. Remove from the oven and immediately remove the biscuits from the tins. Serve warm.

To reheat, wrap muffins in a paper towel and microwave on high for about 30 seconds.

Zucchini Bread

A friend of mine moved back to live on his grandparents' farm in lovely Rembert, South Carolina. Sometime around the first part of June each year, I'll find on my side porch early one morning a large basket of zucchini he's dropped off on his way into the office. Zucchini bread follows shortly thereafter. While it is yummy baked in 5 × 9-inch loaf pans, I love to bake it in muffin tins or brownie pans with multiple wells so I end up with more of the delicious crusty parts.

Makes 2 loaves (serves 16)

- 2 cups freshly grated zucchini, drained in a colander
- 1½ cups granulated sugar
- 1 cup vegetable oil
- 3 whole large eggs, beaten
- 2 teaspoons vanilla extract
- 2 cups all-purpose flour
- 1 tablespoon ground cinnamon
- 1½ teaspoons baking soda
- ½ teaspoon baking powder
- ½ teaspoon salt
- 1 cup chopped pecans or walnuts
- 1 cup raisins

Preheat the oven to 375°F. Grease two 5 × 9-inch baking pans with butter or baking spray with flour.

In a large mixing bowl, combine the zucchini, sugar, oil, eggs, and vanilla. In a separate bowl, sift together the flour, cinnamon, baking soda, baking powder, and salt. Add the dry mixture to wet mixture and mix until well combined.

Stir in the nuts and raisins and transfer the batter to the prepared baking pans. Bake for 1 hour. To test for doneness, gently press the top of each loaf; if they bounce back slightly, they're done. Remove from the oven. Remove the loaves from the pans and set aside on a wire rack to cool. Serve warm.

NOTE: The batter can also be scooped into 3 (2½-inch–12-well) medium muffin tins greased with baking spray with flour. Bake for 25 to 30 minutes, until done.

2

Hors d'Oeuvres

The Case of the Copious Crawfish

Shrimp, crab, and oysters are all staples of Lowcountry cuisine, but crawfish are becoming increasingly available and even commercially raised in South Carolina.

Crawfish were on the menu once at a legislative party many years ago. Three fifty-pound croaker sacks of them arrived for the party, but only half of one bag ended up getting boiled and consumed. That left two and a half bags of claw-clicking, really mad, but still alive, crawfish. Several folks were tasked with disposing of the crawfish in a humane manner. Their first plan—dumping them in the fountain at the governor's mansion—was quickly ruled out as unworkable, as they'd have to be spirited past security, and besides, it was possibly cruel to the crawfish to free them and then leave them in the vicinity of a governor known for being so cheap that he might have fished them out and eaten them!

Plan B was to dump them into the Congaree River at the boat landing off Bluff Road that's located behind the University of South Carolina Gamecocks' practice field near Williams-Brice Stadium. Under the cover of darkness, the team accomplished their mission. Feeling good about freeing the crawfish, they returned to their hotel and went to sleep.

Shortly thereafter, the South Carolina Highway Patrol got a call that crawfish were seen marching across Bluff Road toward the stadium. The Patrol thought it was a crank call from some prankster Carolina students, but they checked it out anyway. Sure enough, there they were—a bunch of mad crawfish crossing the road. A few weeks later, a small article about the incident appeared in *The State* newspaper; apparently, the Department of Natural Resources was at a loss to explain a bumper crop of crawfish—a species not normally seen in this area—in the Congaree River. No one, but no one, breathed a word as to who the culprits might have been.

Live free, little crawfish, live free! Unless, of course, you'd like to show up as appetizers someday.

Crawfish Spread

Below is the base recipe for this delicious spread; it's followed by recipes for red rice cups, mixing it with pasta, and baking it in French bread. It will soon become a favorite in your kitchen.

Makes 36 tarts

- 1 tablespoon unsalted butter
- ½ cup finely chopped onion
- 2 tablespoons thinly sliced green onions
- 3 tablespoons finely chopped celery
- 1 teaspoon minced garlic
- 1 teaspoon salt
- ½ teaspoon Tony Chachere's Original Creole Seasoning
- ¼ teaspoon freshly ground black pepper
- 1 cup cream cheese, softened
- 3 tablespoons red pepper jelly
- 2 tablespoons chopped fresh parsley
- 2 teaspoons soy sauce
- 1 (12-ounce) package crawfish tails, chopped (see note)

Melt the butter in a medium size frying pan over medium heat. Add the onion and green onion and sauté for about 3 minutes. Add the celery and garlic and sauté for 2 minutes more. Remove from the heat and add the salt, Creole seasoning, and black pepper.

Place the cream cheese in a large bowl and pour the warm onion mixture over the top of it. Set aside to allow it to soften. Add the red pepper jelly, parsley, and soy sauce and mix together with a hand or stand mixer on low speed until well blended. Using a spatula, fold in the crawfish.

Cover the bowl with plastic wrap and refrigerate for at least 2 hours. Serve as a dip with crackers or fresh vegetables, as a filling for Red Rice Cups, in Crawfish Pasta, or in Crawfish Bread (recipes follow).

NOTE: For the pasta recipe, only chop half the crawfish.

RED RICE CUPS

- 3 cups Sarah Seabrook's Red Rice (p. 72)
- 1 whole large egg, beaten
- 1 recipe Crawfish Spread (recipe above)

Preheat the oven to 350°F. Grease 3 miniature muffin tins, each with 12 (1¾-inch) wells, with butter or cooking spray.

Place 1½ cups of the rice in the bowl of a food processor and process until the grains are reduced by about half.

Place the remaining 1½ cups of rice in a medium bowl. Add the processed rice and mix well. Add the egg and mix until the rice holds together if pressed into a ball.

Using a #70 scoop or a tablespoon, place the rice in the prepared muffin tins. Press down on the center of each with the back of the scoop, a spoon, or the small end of a melon baller, making a well. Bake for 10 minutes. Remove from the oven and set aside to cool slightly.

Transfer to a serving platter, fill each cup with a dab of the Crawfish Spread, and serve.

NOTE: The Red Rice Cups and Crawfish Spread can be made ahead and refrigerated separately for up to 2 days. Arrange the cups on a baking sheet with sides, cover with foil, and refrigerate. To reheat, place the baking sheet, still covered with foil, in a 250°F oven until warm, about 10 minutes. Fill each with the Crawfish Spread and serve.

CRAWFISH PASTA

Makes 8 servings

- 2 cups dried bowtie or orecchiette pasta
- 1 recipe Crawfish Spread (recipe above)
- Freshly grated Parmesan for serving

When preparing the Crawfish Spread, only chop half the crawfish, leaving other half whole.

Cook the pasta according to package directions. Remove from the heat and drain.

Mix the cooked pasta with the Crawfish Spread. Sprinkle with the Parmesan and serve.

CRAWFISH BREAD

Makes 8 servings

- 1 recipe Crawfish Spread (recipe above)
- 4 ounces sharp white Cheddar, freshly grated
- 4 ounces provolone, freshly grated
- 2 (15-inch) loaves soft French bread, sliced almost in half lengthwise

Preheat the oven to 350°F.

Mix together the Crawfish Spread, Cheddar, and provolone in a medium bowl. Divide the spread evenly between the 2 loaves and press them together slightly to close.

Tightly wrap each loaf in foil, place them on a baking sheet, and bake until the cheese is melted and the bread is heated all the way through, about 25 to 30 minutes. Remove from the oven, cut into 2-inch slices, and serve hot.

Bacon Deviled Eggs

When I was a little girl, I spent the summers in Greer, South Carolina, with my grandmother and Aunt Mary Dob (this was before they moved to Beaufort). Before church each Sunday, Gran-Gran would rise early to make deviled eggs and pimento cheese sandwiches, and Mary Dob would fry up some chicken. After church, we'd come home, pack up all the goodies in a peach basket, and head up Highway 14, eventually making our way to some two-lane mountain roads for a nice Sunday drive. After a while, we'd find a spot beside a stream with a picnic table and spread out our lunch treasures.

From left to right, Aunt Mary Moseley Dobson, Aunt Martha "Mimi" Alice Dobson, Mrs. E. S. Dobson (my grandmother), and my mother, Jean Dobson Greene, pictured at Camp Croft near Spartanburg, SC, during World War II. They were very active in the Red Cross and helped entertain soldiers at the Army base and at my grandmother's home in Greer. I'm sure there's a cake in that cake box Mimi is holding, and a peach basket was always the official picnic basket of my family.

The interstates have long since taken over as the preferred method of transportation for most people, but nothing can top the memories of those beautiful summer Sunday afternoon drives. I think they're why I've loved deviled eggs ever since. I make them all the time for tailgates, and I make sure several dozen are on the table for Jane and Robert Key's annual St. Patrick's Day party and informal Deviled Egg Eating Contest.

While it may seem a little counterintuitive, eggs that are a little bit on the older side (at least a week) are easier to peel. During peak deviled egg season, also known as football tailgating season, I keep a range of eggs of various ages in the refrigerator. If you want the yolks to be perfectly in the center of the eggs, invert the carton the night before you are going to boil them.

Makes 24 halves

14 large eggs

1 tablespoon white vinegar

½ cup bacon bits

¼ cup sweet pickle relish, drained

¼ cup + 2 tablespoons mayonnaise

¼ cup Champagne Mustard (p. 78) or Durkee Famous Sauce

¼ to ½ teaspoon salt

¼ teaspoon freshly ground black pepper

¼ teaspoon smoked paprika plus more for garnish (optional)

Place the eggs in a single layer in a large Dutch oven or stockpot with a lid and cover with 1 inch of water. Add the vinegar (it makes the eggs easier to peel), place over medium-to-high heat, and bring to a boil. Immediately cover, remove from the heat, and set aside for 12 minutes.

Transfer the eggs to a strainer, drain, and return to the Dutch oven. Cover with cold water. Immediately begin to peel each egg by first tapping it on the side of sink and then holding it under warm running water and peeling off all of the shell and membrane (see notes). Transfer to a large platter lined with paper towels to absorb any excess water. Repeat until all the eggs have been peeled. Set aside the two eggs that were most damaged by the peeling process.

Slice each of the remaining dozen eggs in half lengthwise and remove the yolks, transferring them to the bowl of a food processor. Arrange the 24 empty egg white halves on a platter or on deviled egg dishes. Add the 2 whole eggs, the bacon bits, and the relish to the food processor and pulse a few times, until the yolks begin to crumble but are not mushy. Add the remaining ingredients and pulse until well blended, taking care not to overprocess it (it should not be mushy).

Spoon the mixture into a large pastry bag with no tip (see notes). Squeeze the mixture into each egg white half. Garnish each with additional paprika, if desired, and serve.

NOTES: Most kitchen stores sell a little round gadget that pierces the bottom of an egg, making it easier to peel. It's well worth the investment if you love deviled eggs!

To fill the pastry bag, place it in a tall glass, fold the top over the side of the glass, and then spoon the mixture into the bag. If you do not have a pastry bag, place the mixture in a gallon ziplock bag and trim off the bottom corner of the bag. Squeeze the contents of the bag into the egg whites out of the bottom of the bag.

"Cheese and Jelly Stuff"

At a party long ago, my friend's husband dubbed this recipe "Cheese and Jelly Stuff"—as in, "I hope Mary is serving that cheese and jelly stuff." Its real name is the "Plains Cheese Ring," and it was purportedly former First Lady Rosalynn Carter's recipe when she lived in the White House. We've been to Plains, Georgia, many times to hear President Carter teach Sunday school, and although we have had many fun adventures, we have never seen it served when we were there.

The great thing about this recipe, in addition to the fact it's so *easy,* is all the variations you can make using it. Substitutions are listed below.

Makes 1 ring (serves 10 to 12)

- 1 pound freshly grated extra-sharp Cheddar
- 1 cup chopped pecans
- 1 medium onion, grated
- ¾ cup mayonnaise
- ½ teaspoon minced garlic
- ½ teaspoon hot pepper sauce
- 1 cup strawberry preserves
- Fresh strawberries (optional) and crackers for serving

Line a ring mold or Bundt pan with plastic wrap.

Combine the Cheddar, pecans, onion, mayonnaise, garlic, and hot pepper sauce in the bowl of a stand mixer or food processor and mix until blended but not completely smooth. Transfer the mixture to the prepared mold and refrigerate for 4 to 6 hours.

When ready to serve, place a plate on top of the mold and invert it, removing the mold from the ring. Remove the plastic wrap and fill the center with the preserves. Serve garnished with the fresh strawberries, if desired, and the crackers.

NOTE: For other flavors, consider one of these variations: 1. Substitute pineapple preserves for the strawberry preserves and serve in a hollowed-out fresh pineapple, leaving the crown intact. 2. Substitute cashews for the pecans and add ½ teaspoon mild curry powder. Mold in a 9-inch cake pan or a tart pan with a raised edge lined with plastic wrap. Substitute chopped Major Grey's Chutney for the preserves and sprinkle the top with more chopped cashews, grated coconut, and finely sliced green onions. 3. Substitute ½ pound pepper Jack and ½ pound extra-sharp white Cheddar for the extra-sharp Cheddar and red pepper jelly for the strawberry preserves. 4. Substitute fig preserves for the strawberry preserves and sprinkle bacon bits over the preserves.

Crab and Shrimp Bundles

Store-bought wonton wrappers make these tasty seafood treats a cinch to make. They're a great way to use up a little leftover seafood; you can make them and store them in the freezer for later.

Just don't do what former Vice President Walter Mondale did when he visited Beaufort during the 1976 presidential campaign. Bless his heart, he was from Minnesota, but maybe someone from Beaufort should have warned him that you have to peel boiled shrimp before popping them in your mouth. I'll bet he never made that mistake again!

These wontons are ready to pop in your mouth—no peeling needed.

Makes 24 bundles

4 ounces cream cheese, softened

¼ cup crumbled feta cheese

1 green onion, thinly sliced

1 tablespoon Dijon mustard or Champagne Mustard (p. 78)

1 tablespoon dry white wine

1 tablespoon minced fresh parsley

1 cup cooked shrimp, peeled and chopped or crab (or ½ cup each)

24 (3-inch square) wonton wrappers

Preheat the oven to 375°F. Grease 2 miniature muffin tins, each with 12 (1¾-inch) wells, with butter-flavored baking spray.

In a medium bowl, mix together the cream cheese and feta. Add the green onion, mustard, wine, and parsley and stir well. Stir in the shrimp and/or crab.

Place a wonton wrapper in each prepared muffin well and press lightly. Place a heaping teaspoon of the filling mixture in the middle of each wrapper (a #100 scoop works well for this). Fold up the sides and twist to close.

Bake until lightly brown, 12 to 15 minutes. Remove from the oven and serve immediately.

NOTES: The Crab and Shrimp Bundles may also be made ahead and frozen. Make the bundles, place them in muffin tins, and freeze. Once they are frozen solid, remove from tins, transfer them to aluminum trays and wrap well in plastic wrap. When ready to use, place the still-frozen bundles on a baking sheet and bake at 375°F for 15 to 18 minutes.

Although these are wonderful just by themselves, a bowl of the pungent sauce from my recipe for Momma's Fried Shrimp (p. 114) makes a nice addition.

Clemson Blue Cheese, Vidalia Onion, and Bacon Spread

Clemson University—"Where the Blue Ridge yawns its greatness"—has been producing artisanal blue cheese since 1941, when it was cured in the abandoned Stumphouse tunnel. Today, it's cured in a state-of-the-art facility on the Clemson campus and distributed all over the country via overnight shipping at www.Clemson.edu/bluecheese. It's so good, even a diehard University of South Carolina Gamecock fan can like something from Clemson.

This recipe calls for Vidalia onions, but other sweet onions can be substituted. True Vidalia onions are grown in only thirteen counties in Georgia. When they're in season, people buy them by the box. The traditional method for preserving them was to tie them up in a torn pair of panty hose, with a knot between each onion so you can snip them off as you needed them. The hose were hung up in pantries or cellars to be used throughout the year. As interest has waned in both pantries and hose, an alternative method is to wrap each onion in a paper towel and store them in the crisper drawer of your refrigerator. You can also freeze Vidalias while they are in season. First, wash, peel, and chop the onions and spread them on a rimmed baking sheet. Freeze for several hours. Once frozen, store in ziplock bags, placing 1 cup in each bag so they're ready to pull out of the freezer and make this spread.

Makes 5 cups
(serves 8 to 10)

2 (8-ounce) packages cream cheese, at room temperature

8 ounces Clemson Blue Cheese, at room temperature, plus more as desired

1 cup finely chopped Vidalia onions

1 cup bacon bits

½ cup freshly shredded mozzarella

¼ cup freshly shredded Asiago or Parmesan

½ teaspoon garlic powder

½ teaspoon onion powder

Toasted pita points for serving

Preheat the oven to 400°F. Grease an ovenproof serving dish with butter-flavored baking spray.

Combine all of the ingredients except the pita points and mix on medium speed with a hand mixer or stand mixer until well blended. Spoon into the prepared serving dish. Bake until bubbly, about 10 minutes. Remove from the oven and serve with the pita points.

NOTE: The spread may also be served cold but bake it first and allow it to cool so that all the ingredients melt together. If there are any leftovers, a dollop of this spread is very tasty on a beautifully grilled steak.

Individual Tomato Tarts

For about six weeks every summer, St. Helena Island is the tomato capital of the world—or at least of the East Coast. There used to be numerous tomato packing sheds in Beaufort County—Six L's, Seaside, Bishops, Trask's, McLeod's, Scott Farms, and J. O. Youngblood, which canned its "JOY" tomatoes. Working in the packing house as soon as school was out for the summer was a rite of passage for many local teenagers. Sadly, only about three packing houses are left. According to my cousin, a produce broker, if you eat a tomato in a fast-food restaurant on the East Coast in late May or early June, he'll bet you a dime to a dollar that it came from Beaufort County, South Carolina, or at least the South Carolina Lowcountry.

Truth be told, I'm not a big fan of fresh tomatoes—I just don't like the squishy texture. I know that is blasphemy for a girl from my neck of the woods, but at least I've learned to love them cooked so I can enjoy delicious tarts like these. These tomato tarts are an easy summertime treat or a good substitute when you're craving a tomato pie in the dead of winter. Using crescent dough from the refrigerated section at the grocery store is an easy way to make these pies look like they took more work than they really require.

Makes 36 tarts

1 (10-ounce) can Rotel tomatoes (mild or original), well drained

1 cup Duke's mayonnaise (or Miracle Whip, if you must)

½ cup bacon bits

1 cup freshly grated extra-sharp Cheddar

3 (8-ounce) tubes refrigerated crescent roll dough

Preheat the oven to 350°F. Grease 3 miniature muffin tins, each with 12 (1¾-inch) wells, with butter-flavored baking spray.

Combine all of the ingredients except the crescent roll dough in a bowl and mix together. Set aside.

On a floured pastry cloth or a clean work surface dusted with flour, lightly roll out 1 sheet of the crescent roll dough, just enough to make it of a uniform thickness. Cut into 12 (3-inch) circles.

Place the dough circles in the prepared muffin wells and press down. Spoon 1 tablespoon of the filling into each dough cup. Repeat with the remaining 2 tubes of dough.

Bake until golden brown, about 15 minutes. Use a knife to remove the tarts from the muffin tins and transfer to a serving dish. Serve warm.

Frogmore Stew Dip

Frogmore Stew—or Beaufort Stew, as it is also known—is a Lowcountry staple (see p. 118 in Seafood chapter). Once, when I was trying to come up with something different for a spring cocktail party, I turned Frogmore Stew into a party dip. This recipe is also a great way to use up leftovers from an actual stew: just use about half the cream cheese, butter, and Zatarain's, trim the corn off the cob, and chop up any remaining sausage and shrimp until you have at least 3 cups. Last night's supper can be tonight's appetizer!

Makes 8 cups
(serves 12 to 16)

- 1 (16-ounce) package frozen whole kernel corn
- 1 (14-ounce) package Kielbasa sausage
- 1 tablespoon Old Bay seasoning
- 1 pound fresh shrimp, peeled and deveined
- 2 (8-ounce) packages cream cheese, at room temperature
- 8 tablespoons (1 stick) unsalted butter, softened
- 1 teaspoon Zatarain's liquid crab boil
- Fritos, corn chips, or butter-flavored crackers for serving

Preheat the oven to 350°F. Grease a 7 × 11-inch casserole dish with butter or cooking spray.

Thaw the corn in a strainer, allowing any excess water to drain.

Cut the sausage into quarters lengthwise and then chop them into ½-inch pieces.

Cook the sausage in a skillet over medium heat until lightly brown. Remove from the heat and transfer the sausage to a plate lined with paper towels to absorb any excess grease.

Fill a pot with water and add the Old Bay seasoning. Place it over medium heat and bring to a boil. Add the shrimp and boil for 3 to 5 minutes. Remove from the heat, drain, and chop the shrimp into pieces about the same size as sausage. (If a finer chop is desired, the shrimp and sausage can be pulsed several times in the bowl of a food processor.)

Using a hand mixer or stand mixer on medium-high speed, cream together the cream cheese and butter and then add the liquid crab boil. Using a spatula, fold the corn, sausage, and shrimp into the mixture. Transfer the mixture to the prepared casserole dish and bake until heated through and bubbly, 20 to 25 minutes. Remove from the oven and serve warm with the Fritos, chips, or crackers.

"THAT" Dip

I traveled a lot when I worked for the National Education Association affiliate in South Carolina. At conferences, if our hotel rooms had stove tops or microwaves, someone would always ask, "Are you going to make 'THAT' dip?' Because it combines Velveeta with Rotel tomatoes and peppers, it was lovingly dubbed "Redneck Rotel Dip." It was always a big hit.

One year we attended a conference on Sanibel Island in Florida, and I went to an Albertson's in Fort Myers to pick up all the ingredients. I couldn't find the Velveeta, and since the store had a large selection of gourmet cheeses, I wanted to be rather discreet when asking as to its whereabouts. I asked the store manager, who proceeded to get on the store PA system and ask a stock boy to "help the lady in the red shirt find the *Velveeeetter.*" If I could have pulled the floor tiles up and crawled under them, I would have.

More recently I was visiting with friends in Isle of Palms, South Carolina, home of the ritzy Wild Dunes Resort. You know you are somewhere swanky when they have the Velveeta in the refrigerated section of the grocery store right along with the real cheese.

If there are any leftovers, cook up a pot of grits the next morning and stir the leftovers into the grits—yum, yum! Whenever I'm making the dip and am planning to do this for breakfast the next day, I preemptively remove 2 cups of the dip before serving it so we will be sure to have enough. If you try this, cook 1 cup of dried grits for every 2 cups of dip.

Makes 5 cups
(serves 1 to 10, depending on who is eating it!)

- 1 pound bulk sausage (mild or hot)
- 1 (8-ounce) package cream cheese, softened
- 1 (8-ounce) package pasteurized processed cheese (Velveeta)
- 1 (10-ounce) can Rotel undrained tomatoes (mild or original)
- Corn chips for serving

Cook the sausage in a pan over medium heat until lightly brown. Remove from the heat and transfer the sausage to a plate lined with paper towels to absorb any excess grease.

Combine the cream cheese and processed cheese in a large microwave-safe bowl and heat on high for 2 minutes. Stir well and heat on high for 1 minute more. Stir until smooth and add the sausage and tomatoes. Heat on high for 1 minute longer.

Remove from the microwave and stir well. Serve with the corn chips.

NOTE: To turn this into a Tex-Mex dip, add 1 (15-ounce) can drained and rinsed black beans and 1 (15¼-ounce) can drained shoepeg corn. Stir together. (If you're making a Tex-Mex version, don't mix it into grits.)

Rock Shrimp Dip

One year we had a late frost, and most of the shrimp crop was wiped out. Local seafood houses scrambling for something to replace them introduced rock shrimp from Florida, which have a tougher shell and are much harder to peel than our usual brown or white shrimp.

As locals experimented to see if their beloved recipes would work using rock shrimp, my friend Gary Ray Rakestraw came up with this recipe, which we have loved and used all the years since. Trader Joe's carries langostinos, already peeled and cooked, which work as a great substitute for rock shrimp in this recipe. It's equally good with regular shrimp or crab, or a mixture of whatever leftover seafood you may have on hand.

Makes 2 cups (serves 4)

- 1 (8-ounce) package cream cheese
- 3 tablespoons mayonnaise
- 2 teaspoons Champagne Mustard (p. 78) or Durkee Famous Sauce
- 1 cup cooked rock shrimp, peeled and chopped
- 1 tablespoon white wine or sherry
- ½ teaspoon Tony Chachere's Original Creole Seasoning
- Crackers or celery for serving

Combine the cream cheese, mayonnaise, and Champagne Mustard in a large microwave-safe bowl and heat on high for 1 to 2 minutes, until it is easily stirred together.

Remove from the microwave, add the remaining ingredients except the crackers, and stir well. Serve warm with the crackers or celery.

Smoked Gouda and Bacon Pimento Cheese

Once, during a particularly heated legislative battle, we decided to order lunch from the No Name Deli in Columbia. Yes, that's actually the place's name—No Name. Our assistant jotted down our orders as we called them out. My turn came fairly early in the process, and I asked for "a pimento cheese sandwich, toasted, please." After she'd taken down all the orders, I glanced at her list and didn't see my pimento cheese sandwich listed. I inquired just to make sure it was on the list, and she replied, "Oh yes, see, right here . . . MC . . . 'minter cheese."

The following recipe is some powerful good 'minter cheese. You can also experiment with other kinds of cheese by substituting blue cheese or pepper Jack for the Gouda . . . scrumptious!

Makes 4 cups (serves 8)

8 ounces smoked Gouda

8 ounces white Cheddar

4 ounces whipped cream cheese, softened (see note)

½ cup mayonnaise

2 teaspoons sriracha sauce

1 teaspoon Worcestershire sauce

1 teaspoon apple cider vinegar

1 teaspoon dry mustard

½ teaspoon salt

1 (2-ounce) jar diced pimientos, drained

1 cup bacon bits

Crackers, pita chips, or celery for serving

Shred the Gouda and Cheddar together in a bowl. Set aside.

Using a hand mixer or stand mixer on medium speed, beat together the cream cheese, mayonnaise, sriracha, Worcestershire, vinegar, dry mustard, and salt until well blended. Add the grated cheeses, pimientos, and bacon bits. Using a spatula, stir until mixed but not completely smooth. Serve with the crackers, pita chips, or celery.

NOTE: You can omit the cream cheese and add an extra ½ cup of mayonnaise, if preferred.

Savory Blue Cheese Cheesecake

When my two eldest godchildren, Windy and Sally, were young we used to make these cheesecakes in 4-inch individual springform pans as Christmas gifts for the girls' teachers. My mother and grandmother had been teachers, and I lobbied for the teachers' association in South Carolina for many years. If there's one thing I know for sure, it's that teachers don't need another coffee mug or Christmas ornament that says, "World's Best Teacher."

The girls and I would make the cheesecakes, wrap them in cellophane, tie on a palmetto tree spreader, and pop them in the freezer. On the last day of school, the girls would take them out of the freezer and bring them to school, and by the time their teachers got home that night, the cheesecakes would be thawed and ready to eat with a glass of wine to celebrate the beginning of Christmas break. When Sally Key went off to college at Clemson, I asked her if we still needed to make them for her college professors—after all, we made them with Clemson Blue Cheese. She told me she thought she was a little old for teachers' gifts. (But I'll bet they would have loved them!)

Makes 1 (9-inch), 3 (6-inch), or 6 (4-inch) savory cheesecake(s) (serves 20 to 25)

15 garlic-flavored Ritz crackers

¼ cup grated Parmesan

½ pound (8 to 10 slices) bacon or 1 cup bacon bits

1 medium onion, finely chopped

3½ (8-ounce) packages cream cheese, softened

4 whole large eggs

½ cup heavy cream

½ pound Clemson Blue Cheese

½ teaspoon salt

¼ teaspoon dried basil

(*continued*)

Preheat the oven to 300°F. Line the bottom of 1 (9-inch), 3 (6-inch), or 6 (4-inch) springform pan(s) with foil. Grease the pan(s) and foil with butter or butter-flavored baking spray.

Pulse the crackers in the bowl of a food processor until crushed and add the Parmesan and pulse again. Spread the cracker mixture in the bottom of each pan. Press lightly with back of a spoon until a crust forms.

Tear off 2 sheets of foil per springform pan and stack one on top of the other, turning one so that together, they form an 8-point star. Set each springform pan in the center of the foil star and roll the foil around each pan, forming a collar that will prevent water from seeping in. Set aside.

Fry the bacon in a pan over medium-low heat until crispy but not overcooked. Remove from the heat and transfer the bacon to a plate lined with paper towels to

¼ teaspoon crushed dried rosemary

¼ teaspoon freshly ground black pepper

2–3 drops hot pepper sauce

Crackers or pita chips for serving

absorb any excess grease. Crumble the bacon and set aside.

Drain all but 1 tablespoon of the bacon drippings from the pan. Return to medium heat, add the onion, and cook for 5 to 10 minutes, or until translucent. Remove from the heat.

Using a hand mixer or stand mixer on medium-high speed, blend the cream cheese, eggs, and cream until light and fluffy. Add the crumbled bacon, cooked onion, Clemson Blue Cheese, salt, basil, rosemary, black pepper, and hot pepper sauce to the mixture and mix on medium speed until well combined.

Transfer the mixture to each prepared springform pan on top of the crust.

Set the springform pan(s) with foil collar(s) inside a larger roasting pan with at least 2-inch sides. Fill the roasting pan with 1 inch of very hot water.

If baking 1 (9-inch) cheesecake, bake for 1 hour and 40 minutes. If baking 3 (6-inch) cheesecakes, bake for 1 hour and 30 minutes. If baking 6 (4-inch) cheesecakes, bake for 1 hour and 10 minutes. Remove each springform pan from the roasting pan, remove from foil collar and set aside to cool at room temperature for 2 hours, and then refrigerate overnight.

To release the cheesecake(s) from the pan(s), run a knife around the edge of the pan. Release the side of the pan(s) and remove. Peel foil from crust and place cheesecake on a plate or cake round covered in foil. Serve with the crackers or pita chips.

Shrimp and Grits Tarts

Years ago, when I wanted something new to serve at my annual Twelfth Night party, I created these all-in-one shrimp and grits tarts. They were such a hit at the party that I submitted them to a recipe contest for *Southern Living* magazine . . . and heard nothing! Imagine my surprise later that fall when I flipped through *Southern Living*'s annual holiday issue and found inside my recipe, complete with a picture. I don't think my mother could have ever been prouder of something I'd done.

My mother was in a group loosely referred to as the Coffee Club—eleven of her nearest and dearest friends who met every Wednesday morning for coffee, a light lunch, and an "information exchange." The Coffee Club members, who had all received their copies of *Southern Living* that week, were distraught to find my name listed as Mary M. Greene, which was what I used professionally, rather than Mary Martha Greene, and they thought my home should be have been listed as Beaufort, South Carolina, not Columbia—even though I had lived in Columbia for twenty-five years.

Several years later, we attended an engagement party at a gorgeous home on the Tennessee River in Knoxville, Tennessee. As servers passed trays of food, my friends and I suddenly realized they were serving my shrimp and grits tarts! I asked a young server where the recipe had come from; she told me that she didn't know, but the caterer was in the kitchen if I'd like to talk to her. I was dying to see the kitchen anyway, so of course I asked to meet her. The caterer, who hemmed and hawed and swore that she didn't remember where she'd gotten the recipe. I replied that she'd gotten it from *Southern Living;* it was my recipe; and that they should be served hot, not lukewarm or cold, like she was serving them. The next tray that came around was hot, so I took that as her admission that it was my recipe.

Makes 36 tarts

- 36 medium-to-large fresh shrimp, peeled and deveined
- 36 Grits Tarts (recipe follows)
- ½ recipe Tasso Gravy, omitting the coffee (p. 112)
- Chopped fresh parsley for garnish

Preheat the oven to 350°F.

Fill a large saucepan halfway full with water. Place it over medium heat and bring to a boil. Add the shrimp and boil for 2 to 3 minutes, until light pink. Remove from the heat and drain.

Arrange the Grits Tarts on a baking sheet with sides. Place 1 teaspoon Tasso Gravy in each tart and top each with a shrimp. Bake for 5 to 10 minutes. Remove from the oven, garnish tarts with fresh parsley, and serve warm.

GRITS TARTS

- 2 cups chicken broth
- 1 cup whole milk
- 2 tablespoon unsalted butter
- 1 cup coarsely ground grits
- 1 teaspoon salt
- ½ teaspoon white pepper
- ⅔ cup grated Parmesan

Preheat the oven to 350°F. Grease 3 miniature muffin tins, each with 12 (1¾-inch) wells, liberally with butter-flavored baking spray.

Bring the broth, milk, and butter to a medium boil in a large saucepan over medium heat. Once the mixture boils, add the grits, salt, and white pepper, whisking constantly to make sure the grits do not become lumpy. Reduce the heat to low and cook according to package directions until the mixture thickens and the grits are done. Remove from the heat and whisk in the Parmesan until melted.

Spoon 1 tablespoon of the grits mixture into each muffin well using a tablespoon measure or a #70 scoop. Spray each dollop of the grits mixture with the cooking spray. Using the small round end of a melon baller or a spoon, press down on the center of each, making a small indentation.

Bake for 20 to 25 minutes. Remove from the oven and, while the tarts are still warm, press down on the center of each again with the melon baller. Set aside at room temperature and let tarts cool for 10 to 15 minutes. Remove the tarts from the muffin tins by running a dull knife around the edges, if necessary.

NOTE: The tarts can be prepared ahead to this point, placed on a baking sheet with sides, covered in plastic wrap, and stored for 2 to 3 days in the refrigerator. The tarts can also be filled with the Tasso Gravy ahead of time and refrigerated. To reheat, place them on a baking sheet covered with foil and warm them in a 350°F oven for 10 minutes.

Oyster Sausage Cocktail Bites

This recipe is from Elizabeth's on 37th, a fabulous restaurant in Savannah, Georgia. The original pastries were much larger, intended to be served in appetizer portions, but I adapted them into cocktail party bites. Aunt Mimi always referred to these as "beggar's purses," I think because people always begged for more.

When I entertain, I always like to make individual servings of appetizers so that people can easily pick them up and place them on a plate. This can be particularly important if you don't have a large dining room—you need to serve things people can pick up that will allow them to move on. This will help with the flow of your party.

One of my mother's most important rules of entertaining was to be at the door to greet your guests for any type of party. She always said you should be the first person a guest sees when they arrive and the last one they see as they leave. I try to follow her rule.

My second rule is to have some food for guests to pick up as soon as they come through the door—as stated above, something they can pick up and then move on.

My third rule is to put the bar as far away from the front door as possible, so people will move around the house and mingle with other guests. Based on the way my house in Columbia is set up, I always put a bar on my back porch, and I have a bar on the desk in my bedroom! One of the most important rules of entertaining is to figure out ways to use your entire home.

Nathalie Dupree, the queen of Southern cooking, once wrote an article entitled, "What to Eat When Party Hosts Send You Home Hungry?" I told her that I'd die of embarrassment if anyone *ever* left a party at my house hungry.

One of Mother's other rules was to always use plates at a cocktail party. Over many years of standing around and talking at legislative cocktail receptions, I have even mastered the *three-finger plate hold* . . . the art of balancing a plate on your left index and middle finger and securing it on top with your thumb, leaving your ring finger and pinky free to hold your wine glass. Giving your guests a small plate to use at the party is an important part of the pick-it-up-and-move-along plan to rotate people through your dining room.

I try to make sure I serve some substantial food, so guests can make a meal of it if they so choose. I usually serve several seafood dishes; something with chicken or beef; some sort of vegetable, whether it is a tray of raw vegetables or steamed asparagus with a Parmesan peppercorn dressing; fresh strawberries, if they're in season, and an array of individual sweets for dessert, of course. Somehow, the desserts always disappear first.

There's one more rule for entertaining in the South—turn on your air conditioning. I don't care how cold it is outside: if you have a lot of people in your house, with all that body heat, it's going to get hot. There's nothing worse than standing around at a cocktail party in all your finery and sweating like a rented mule. When you get up on the morning of the party, either turn it on or turn it down!

Makes 50 cocktail bites

- ½ pound bulk mild Italian sausage
- ½ cup finely chopped onion
- ½ pint (1 cup) shucked fresh oysters, drained
- ½ cup freshly grated extra sharp Cheddar
- ½ cup freshly grated mozzarella
- 1 (17-ounce) package frozen puff pastry, thawed (see note)

Brown the sausage and onion in a skillet over medium-high heat. Drain the oysters in a colander. Add the oysters to sausage mixture and cook for 2 to 3 minutes, until the edges of the oysters begin to curl. Remove from the heat and return to colander to drain again.

Transfer the contents of the pan to the bowl of a food processor and pulse several times until blended and easier to place in bundles. Set aside to cool to room temperature. Add the Cheddar and mozzarella and stir well.

On a floured pastry cloth or a clean work surface dusted with flour, unfold the puff pastry. Roll out 1 sheet into a 15-inch square. Cut the pastry into 25 (3-inch) squares (yes, I actually pull out a yard stick and measure it) and place a teaspoon of oyster mixture in the center of each square (use a #110 scoop to make sure each portion is roughly equal). Gather the 4 corners of each pastry together and pinch to form a 1-inch square pastry. (Seal each bundle, if desired, by dipping your fingers in a small bowl of water and running them along the edges.) Place each finished bundle on a baking sheet. Repeat with the remaining sheet of pastry. Freeze for 1 hour. (After the bundles are completely frozen, they can be stored in ziplock bags in the freezer for several weeks.)

Preheat the oven to 400°F. Grease a baking sheet with cooking spray or line it with parchment paper.

Place the frozen bundles on the prepared baking sheet, spacing them about 1 inch apart. Bake until golden brown, about 20 minutes. Serve immediately.

NOTE: Sheets of crescent roll dough can be substituted for the puff pastry. Roll each sheet out slightly and cut them into 3-inch squares. Wonton wrappers may be used as well; follow the directions for the Crab and Shrimp Bundles on p. 25.

Smoked Salmon Cheesecake

For many years, I have held my annual Christmas party on January 6th—Twelfth Night, or the traditional twelfth day of Christmas. It's my night to have a party because the Christmas and New Year's seasons are over, and there's not a lot of competition for other events that night. This savory cheesecake is always on the menu.

Shortly after I renovated my kitchen, *The State* newspaper ran a story about my infamous Twelfth Night party that appeared in print right before the party was to occur. My kitchen was done in a rooster and chicken motif, a nod to my beloved Gamecocks, and I didn't want everyone bringing me a bunch of new chicken tchotchkes (pronounced chot-skis). Instead, I decided to ask each of my guests to bring an item to donate to the Columbia Women's Shelter. I contacted the shelter's executive director, who gave me a list of needed items—lotions, journals, laundry supplies, coffee, cream, and sugar. I printed the suggested list on the back of the invitation. Everyone thought it was a great idea and loved bringing something to share with the ladies. I also put out a basket to allow folks who hadn't had time to get to the store to buy something to make a contribution.

Over the years, we've donated tickets to the zoo and the movies and bus passes for the Women's Shelter residents. We've contributed gift cards so they can buy work-related items or cleaning supplies for the house—whatever the greatest need was for that year. It's become a fun tradition that's expanded the fundraising base of the Women's Shelter, as many friends have written checks, and it's given the Women's Shelter more exposure to people who may not have been aware of the wonderful work they perform.

So, pick a favorite charity and give your next party a purpose—canned goods for the food pantry; scarves, gloves, and pullovers for the homeless; art supplies for children's therapy programs; pet food and treats for the animal shelter—whatever tugs at your heart. It will give your guests an extra sense of joy the night of the party and make the afterglow last a little longer when you deliver the goodies to your chosen charity.

Makes 1 (9-inch) or 6 (4-inch) cheesecake(s) (serves 20 to 25)

15 butter-flavored crackers (Ritz or Townhouse brand), plus more for serving

1½ cups freshly grated Parmesan

3 tablespoons unsalted butter, melted

1 large onion, chopped

4 (8-ounce) packages cream cheese, softened

1 cup sour cream

4 whole large eggs

8 ounces smoked salmon, chopped but reserving a few full strips for the top of cake

1 tablespoon dried parsley

1 tablespoon freshly squeezed lemon juice

Freshly grated zest of 1 lemon

2 teaspoons fresh or ¾ teaspoon dried dill

½ teaspoon salt

¼ teaspoon freshly ground black pepper

Crackers for serving

Additional smoked salmon strips, lemon wedges, and fresh dill for garnish

Preheat the oven to 350°F. Line the bottom of 1 (9-inch) or 6 (4-inch) springform pan(s) with foil. Grease the pan(s) and foil with butter-flavored baking spray.

Tear off 2 sheets of foil per springform pan and stack one on top of the other, turning one so that together, they form an 8-point star. Set each springform pan in the center of the foil star and roll the foil around each pan, forming a collar that will prevent water from seeping in. Pulse the crackers in the bowl of a food processor until crushed and add ½ cup of the Parmesan. Spread the cracker mixture in the bottom of each pan. Set aside.

Press lightly with back of a spoon until a crust forms. Melt the butter in a small skillet over medium heat. Add the onion and cook for about 5 minutes, until tender and just starting to brown. Remove from the heat.

Using a hand mixer or stand mixer on medium-high speed, cream together the cream cheese and sour cream until smooth. Add the eggs and blend until smooth. Add the chopped salmon, parsley, lemon juice and zest, dill, salt, and black pepper and mix well. Transfer the mixture to each prepared springform pan on top of the crust. Arrange the reserved full strips of salmon on top of the cheesecake(s) and garnish with more fresh dill, if desired.

Set the springform pan(s) inside a larger roasting pan with at least 2-inch sides. Fill the roasting pan with 1½ inches of very hot water.

If baking 1 (9-inch) cheesecake, bake for 1 hour. If baking 6 (4-inch) cheesecakes, bake for 50 minutes. In either case, turn off the oven and leave the cheesecake(s) in the closed oven for 1 hour more. Remove each springform pan from the roasting pan, remove foil collar and set aside to cool at room temperature for 2 hours, and then refrigerate overnight.

To release the cheesecake(s) from the pan(s), run a knife around the edge of the pan. Release the sides of the pan and remove the foil from the bottom of the cheesecake. Serve cold with the crackers and garnish with the smoked salmon strips, lemon wedges, and fresh dill.

Party Pecans

When I was a child, my mother would make what she called "scrabble" and place it in the center of the beautiful candy trays we gave to friends each Christmas. Today, we call it party mix. It was a major offense to be caught picking the pecans out of my mother's scrabble, so here's the solution: make a big batch of just pecans all for yourself!

Makes 2½ cups

- 3 tablespoons unsalted butter
- 1½ teaspoons Worcestershire sauce
- ½ teaspoon celery salt
- ¼ teaspoon onion powder (not onion salt)
- ¼ teaspoon garlic powder (not garlic salt)
- 2½ cups pecan halves

Preheat the oven to 275°F. Line a rimmed baking sheet with foil and grease with butter-flavored baking spray.

Melt the butter in a small saucepan over medium heat. Add the Worcestershire sauce and seasonings and stir well. Add the pecans and stir, making sure all halves are well coated.

Spread the pecans in a single layer on the prepared baking sheet. Bake on the middle rack of the oven for 30 minutes, stirring every 10 minutes. Remove from the oven and set aside to cool at room temperature for 1 hour. Serve or store in an airtight container for up to 3 weeks.

3

Salads, Vegetables, and Side Dishes

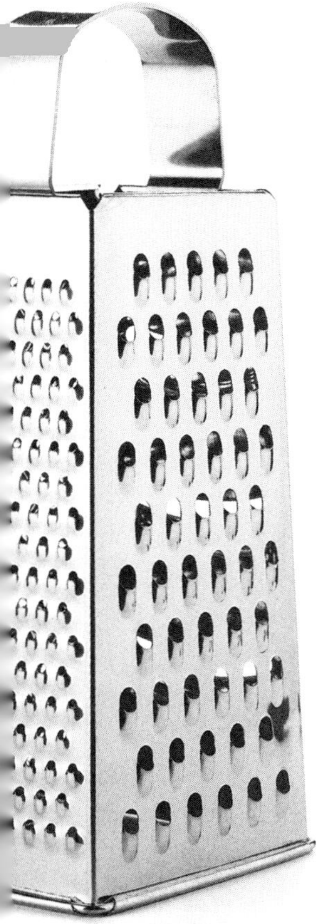

The Great Beaufort County Voter Suppression Scandal of 2008

I come from a long line of Democrats. I am pretty sure my daddy went to his grave without ever voting for a Republican, and I'm pretty sure my mother only ever voted for one in her entire life.

In the late summer of 2008, shortly after her ninety-sixth birthday, my Aunt Mary began a long, slow fade into what was to be her final year. My mother and aunts were all living together in my grandmother's house in Beaufort, and at the time I spent just about every weekend down there with them—or at least two out of every three. Aunt Mary had several health issues: she'd been struggling with scoliosis for many years and was *very* hard of hearing, even with her hearing aids.

In October of that year, Aunt Mary suffered a fall that landed her in a Savannah hospital for a few days. Afterward, we got her back home and settled in. A few days later as I was leaving to return to Columbia, Aunt Mimi asked, "Will you do just one more thing for me before you go?"

Well, Mimi's "one more thing" was to "run" down to the Beaufort County Voter Registration Office and pick up their absentee ballot applications. Normally, this wouldn't have been a problem, except that this was 2008, a time when people were standing in line for two or three *hours* to vote absentee, and I needed to get back to Columbia. I told Mimi to gather up all three of their voter registration cards, call the voter registration office, and ask them to mail a set of absentee ballot request forms to them—and that I'd return to help complete them. Mimi agreed.

The following Sunday, after fixing them a huge dinner that also provided plenty of leftovers for the next week, I sat at the kitchen table with all three of them, eating with one hand and going through paperwork with the other. Insurance papers had come in from Aunt Mary's hospitalization, the flood insurance was due on the house—there were a lot of things to be done. As I neared the end of the stack, I came to their absentee ballot request forms. Mother's was on top, so I checked the box for her to vote absentee because she was over sixty-five and handed the paper off to my right for her to sign. Next up, Aunt Mimi, same drill: I handed the paper across the table for her to sign.

I looked down at the next page, expecting to see Aunt Mary's there as well—and it wasn't there. It was just a little thing, but at that point, I had about one nerve left. I was just done. I looked at my mother and asked, somewhat rhetorically, "Why didn't they send Aunt Mary an absentee ballot form?"

My mother replied, "Well, she was going to vote for John McCain, so we just didn't order her one."

I said, incredulously, "Mother, she's ninety-six years old. This may very well be the last election she ever votes in. Let her vote for whomever she wants."

My mother bowed up in her chair, looked at me over her glasses, and said, "If she's not going to vote 'right,' she's just not going to get to vote!"

The entire time, Aunt Mary just sat there, oblivious to the whole conversation. It just wasn't a hill I was willing to die on that day, so I let it go.

I told this story to the late, great Robert Adams, a friend of mine who once worked for the Republican National Committee and ran many Republican campaigns over the years. He said he was going to call CNN to report *The Great Beaufort County Voter Suppression Scandal of 2008,* and that they'd send Anderson Cooper to investigate.

Well now, Aunt Mimi, like most every other little old lady in America, *loved* her some Anderson Cooper. I told Robert that if Anderson showed up, Aunt Mimi would just barely crack open the front door and say, "Now honey, I don't have any comment about that, but if you'd like to come in and have some sweet tea and cheese biscuits, why, we'd just love to have you."

To the best of my knowledge, Aunt Mary never realized that she didn't get to vote. But it did turn out to be the last election for them all. And that one Republican my mother ever voted for? She drug herself and her oxygen tank out on a cold and rainy Saturday in February 2000 to vote for John McCain in the South Carolina Republican presidential primary!

Triple Bean Bake

When a group of military wives in Beaufort decided to put together a cookbook, they requested recipes from several elected officials. Senator John McCain sent a recipe for Arizona Baked Beans, which can be found in a quick online search. In his memory, here's *my* favorite recipe for baked beans.

Makes 6 to 8 servings

½ pound thick-cut bacon

1 pound lean ground beef

½ cup chopped onion

½ cup packed light brown sugar

¼ cup ketchup

¼ cup barbeque sauce of your choice

2 tablespoons molasses

2 tablespoons prepared yellow or Dijon mustard

1 tablespoon apple cider vinegar

1 tablespoon chili powder

1 teaspoon salt

1 teaspoon freshly ground black pepper

1 (15-ounce) can black beans, drained and rinsed

1 (16-ounce) can baby lima beans, drained

1 (16-ounce) can kidney beans, drained

Preheat the oven to 350°F. Grease a 3-quart ovenproof casserole dish with butter or cooking spray.

Cut the bacon in half lengthwise and then dice into ½-inch pieces. Fry the bacon, stirring often, in a large skillet over medium heat until the bacon is crispy but not overdone. Remove from the heat and, using a slotted spatula, transfer the bacon to a plate lined with paper towels to drain. Set aside. Drain the bacon grease from the skillet.

Return the skillet to the heat and add the ground beef. Brown the beef, using a spatula to break it up as it cooks. Add the onion and cook until the onion is translucent and the beef is fully cooked. Remove from the heat. Transfer the mixture to a plate lined with paper towels to drain.

In a large bowl, combine the brown sugar, ketchup, barbeque sauce, molasses, mustard, vinegar, chili powder, salt, and black pepper. Stir together until blended. Add all the beans and ground beef and stir well.

Transfer the contents of the bowl to the prepared casserole dish and sprinkle the bacon over the top. Bake for 1 hour. Remove from the oven and serve hot.

Calico Vegetables

An old Yiddish saying goes, "Man plans, and God laughs." Aunt Mimi and I always assumed that since she was the youngest, that she'd be the last of the Dobson sisters to survive. We'd planned that if she needed to, she could come live with me in Columbia. My girlfriends joked that she'd be joining us for happy hour and "oohing" and "aahing" over everyone's latest shoes and fashions well into her nineties. Well, God laughed.

Aunt Mary was the first of the sisters to fall seriously ill. When she was sent home with hospice and given only a few weeks to live, Aunt Mimi and my mother dutifully cared for her until one morning, while sitting at the breakfast table, Aunt Mimi had a massive stroke and passed away ten days later. She'd been the one that ran everything in the house—cooked, drove, and did the grocery shopping. Life for all of us changed in an instant.

Sometimes it's the littlest things that are the hardest to deal with when suffering a great loss. With Aunt Mimi gone, I tried to maintain my mother and Aunt Mary at their home in Beaufort, which was their wish. My mother was insistent on having a green vegetable for lunch and dinner every day, so this recipe was a lifesaver for me during that time—it makes a lot and keeps very well. Whenever I had to head back to Columbia, I'd leave a big bowl of it in the refrigerator and voilà—green vegetables on demand. It's also a great side dish for the summer, since you don't have to heat up the stove to make it.

Makes 10 to 12 servings

1 (15-ounce) can small green peas

1 (14½-ounce) can French cut green beans

1 (13-ounce) can sliced mushrooms

1 (11-ounce) can shoepeg corn

1 (4-ounce) jar diced pimientos

1 medium red onion, chopped

1 green or red bell pepper, chopped

2 stalks celery, finely chopped

1 cup apple cider vinegar

¾ cup granulated sugar

½ cup vegetable oil

1 teaspoon salt

½ teaspoon freshly ground black pepper

Drain the peas, green beans, mushrooms, corn, and pimientos in a colander. In a large bowl, mix the drained vegetables with the onion, bell pepper, and celery. In a separate bowl, mix together the vinegar, sugar, oil, salt, and black pepper. Pour the marinade over vegetables and stir gently. Cover with plastic wrap and store overnight in refrigerator, stirring 2 to 3 times while they are marinating. Serve using a slotted spoon; will keep for up to 1 week in the refrigerator.

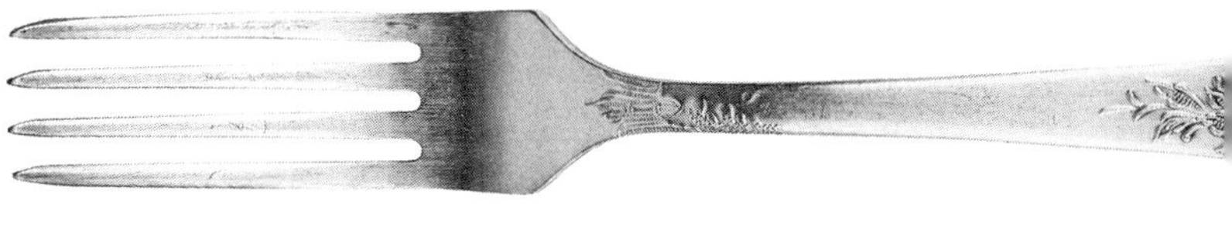

Bean and Corn Salad

When I inherited the Beaufort house, my friend and contractor from Columbia, Jim O'Keefe, came down and renovated it for me. He lived in the house for five months while working on it. Every evening, he sent pictures of the work he'd completed that day, and the title of the email would always be "Today in Paradise." One weekend, Jim's wife and some other friends came down to enjoy a weekend in "paradise" and brought along this bean salad. The cilantro and lime dressing give a little hint of the tropics, so maybe it's a little "taste of paradise" all its own.

Makes 8 servings

SALAD

1 tablespoon extra-virgin olive oil

1 (15¼-ounce) can white shoepeg corn, drained, or 1 cup fresh corn, removed from cob (about 2 ears)

¼ to ½ cup chopped each red, green, and yellow bell pepper

4 to 5 green onions, thinly sliced

2 (15-ounce) cans black beans, rinsed and drained

½ cup minced fresh cilantro

1 cup cherry tomatoes, halved (optional)

1 small avocado, diced (optional)

DRESSING

½ cup balsamic vinegar

3 tablespoons freshly squeezed lime juice

1 teaspoon ground cumin

1 teaspoon salt

½ teaspoon freshly ground black pepper or to taste

Make the Salad: Warm the oil in a skillet over medium-to-high heat. Add the corn (if using fresh), bell peppers, and green onions, and cook until they just begin to brown. About 5 to 10 minutes. Remove from the heat.

Combine the beans and cilantro in a large serving bowl. Add the contents of the skillet and the corn (if using canned) and mix well.

Make the Dressing: Combine the vinegar, lime juice, cumin, salt, and black pepper in a jar. Tightly seal the jar and shake well.

Pour the dressing over the bean mixture and toss until well coated. Add the tomatoes and avocado, if using, and chill for at least 2 hours (the salad can be made up to a day ahead; just add tomatoes and avocado right before serving). Serve cold.

Marinated Asparagus

This is a great side dish, especially for hot summer days when you want to make things in the cooler part of the day and have them on hand. It is a wonderful accompaniment to the Caramelized Vidalia Onion and Bacon Tart (p. 58), along with a freshly sliced St. Helena Island tomato.

Makes 8 servings

2 pounds fresh asparagus or 2 (15-ounce) cans asparagus

½ cup granulated sugar

¼ cup apple cider vinegar

¼ cup water

3 whole cloves

1 stick cinnamon

½ teaspoon celery seed

½ teaspoon salt

If using fresh asparagus, place them on a round rack in the bottom of a Dutch oven or other round pot. Pour water in the bottom of the pot, but do not let the water reach the level of the rack. Place the pot over medium heat and bring the water to a boil. Cook for 3 minutes. Remove from the heat and plunge the asparagus into a sink or bowl filled with ice water to stop the cooking process. Drain and place the asparagus in a shallow bowl or a ziplock bag.

Combine the remaining ingredients in a small saucepan over medium heat. Bring to a boil and cook until the sugar is completely dissolved. Pour the contents of the saucepan over the asparagus and refrigerate for 6 to 24 hours (will keep in the refrigerator for up to 1 week). Serve cold.

Broccoli (or Green Bean) Casserole

Yeah, yeah, I know—everyone knows how to cook this dish, but I need to make sure you know how *not* to cook it!

When my brother George was in high school and I was in junior high, our friend Debbie Spigener (Hamilton) invited our family to dinner. Debbie was a first-year teacher who my mother had taken under her wing. She was also a newlywed who was anxious to use all her wedding presents to create a lovely dinner party, which she beautifully accomplished. She made this broccoli casserole that night, and George fell in love with it. It became part of his cooking repertoire, often on the menus of his special-occasion dinners.

Fast forward many years: A twenty-something friend of George's who had the dish often at his house was dating a young lady he wanted to impress by cooking dinner. He called George to get the recipe, and George dutifully gave it to him over the phone. Several days later, George inquired of the young man how dinner went. Was the young lady duly impressed?

"Well, not exactly," the young man sheepishly replied. He hadn't understood that when George said "a small can of milk," he meant the evaporated kind, NOT sweetened condensed milk, which is what he used. Now, I would eat just about anything with sweetened condensed milk poured over it, but can you imagine anything much nastier than broccoli and cream of mushroom soup combined with sweetened condensed milk?

So, when you make this popular favorite, please follow the directions carefully!

Makes 6 to 8 servings

2 (10-ounce) packages frozen broccoli

1 (10½-ounce) can cream of mushroom soup

1 cup freshly grated sharp Cheddar

1 (5-ounce) can *evaporated* milk

1 ⅓ cups of French's fried onion rings

Preheat the oven to 400°F. Grease a 2-quart casserole dish with butter.

Cook the broccoli according to package directions and drain.

Mix the soup, cheese, and *evaporated* milk together in a large bowl. Add the broccoli and mix well.

Transfer the contents of the bowl to the prepared casserole dish. Bake for 15 minutes. Remove from the oven and sprinkle the fried onions on top. Return to the oven and bake for 5 minutes more. Remove from the oven and serve hot.

NOTE: To make this a green bean casserole, substitute 2 cans drained green beans for the broccoli, but still do *not* use sweetened condensed milk!

Cabbage Bomb

This is my cousin Bill Lamar's recipe. Bill is an avid hunter and often cooks at the hunt club for his fellow hunters. Bill's mother was my eldest first cousin, Patty Dobson Lamar. While Patty was always stylishly dressed, could decorate a lovely home, and set a beautiful table, anyone who knew her would tell you she wasn't much of a cook. If we were planning a party or get together for our circle of friends, we always made sure Patty oversaw bringing the drinks or the paper products, which were always exquisite!

Patty Lamar's next-door neighbor, Patty McDougall, ran the Happy Cookers catering company in Columbia for many years. When the Columbia Junior League was preparing to publish its cookbook *Putting on the Grits,* Patty McDougall gave Patty Lamar several of her best recipes to put in the cookbook. We all wondered if anyone ever tried the truly fabulous recipes that belonged to Patty McDougall, because Patty Lamar's lack of cooking skills was so legendary that everyone might have assumed the recipes weren't very good!

Patty Lamar's former husband (Bill's dad), Billy Lamar, loved to tell the story of the time Patty actually burned salad. When they were newly married and she was preparing dinner one night in the tiny kitchen of their first apartment, she set the tossed salad down on the stove in plastic bowls that promptly melted from the heat. Billy recounted another time when Patty had planned to make Country Captain, a curried chicken dish that contained onions and peppers. She cut up the vegetables and then wrapped them in plastic wrap until it was time to cook them. When she added the vegetables to the dish, some of the plastic wrap got a little too close to the pan and melted into it. Patty just stirred it into the dish. Billy, a dutiful newlywed who didn't want to hurt Patty's feelings, ate it the first night. By the next night, his stomach was torn up from eating the melted plastic wrap the night before. When Patty pulled the leftovers out to reheat them, he suddenly decided they should go out to dinner.

Patty's son Bill, however, is a wonderful cook. This cabbage bomb is great for any outdoor activity—a barbeque, Frogmore Stew, or an oyster roast. It's also fun to cut into wedges and put on the table or the counter for guests to snack on.

Makes 8 to 10 servings, depending on the size of the cabbage

1 large head green cabbage

½ cup apple cider vinegar

Tony Chachere's Original Creole Seasoning or Old Bay seasoning

Salt and freshly ground black pepper to taste

4 strips bacon

Preheat the oven to 350°F. Line a 9 × 13-inch pan or sided baking sheet with foil. Roll up an 18-inch piece of foil lengthwise and then roll it into a circle, forming a crown. Place the crown on top of the baking sheet.

Turn the cabbage upside down, so the core is on top. Using a sharp chef's knife, cut away the core, about 2 to 3 inches deep and wide, and discard it (if the outer leaves start to pull away, secure them with toothpicks). Using a chef's knife, cut slits down into the hole made in the cabbage to allow the other ingredients to seep down into the cabbage.

Place the cabbage on top of the crown. Pour the vinegar into the cabbage a little at a time, allowing it to be fully absorbed. Sprinkle the opening with the desired seasoning of your choice and the salt and black pepper.

Fry the bacon in a pan over medium heat until crispy but not overcooked. Remove from the heat and transfer the bacon to a plate lined with paper towels to absorb any excess grease (reserve the bacon grease). Crumble the bacon and set aside.

Once the vinegar has absorbed into the cabbage, pour the hot bacon grease into the cabbage a little at a time, allowing it to be fully absorbed. Pack the crumbled bacon into the hole.

Bake until the cabbage cuts through easily with a knife, 1½ to 2 hours. Remove from the oven. Cut the cabbage into wedges and either serve in wedges or place on the table to be picked at for a side dish.

NOTE: The cabbage can also be wrapped in foil and cooked in a smoker for 3 hours at 225°F or placed in hot coals for several hours while you are smoking a whole hog.

Caramelized Vidalia Onion and Bacon Tart

This can be a great main course for a summer luncheon. I'm sure Mother and Aunt Mimi served it for their Coffee Club, a group of ladies who met every Wednesday morning for almost fifty years. They met promptly at 11:00 a.m. at one of the twelve members' homes and shared lunch, dessert, coffee, and a little information exchange regarding the town's weekly events (some might say gossip, but they never would have admitted to that). By the time Mother and Mimi met for coffee in the morning and Mimi played bridge that afternoon, there was not much going on in Beaufort worth knowing about that had not been discussed.

Mother served this dish with marinated asparagus or copper carrot pennies. This is also a tasty accompaniment to summer steaks on the grill. If you plan to serve it as a side, you can omit the bacon, but really, why would you? If you want to be able to make it year-round, see the directions for storing Vidalia onions on p. 26.

Makes 6 to 8 servings

- 1 (9-inch) premade deep-dish pie shell
- 8 strips bacon
- 1 teaspoon unsalted butter
- 2 medium Vidalia onions, thinly sliced
- 6 sage leaves, thinly sliced, plus more for garnish
- 3 whole large eggs
- ¾ cup half-and-half
- ¾ teaspoon salt
- 1 teaspoon freshly ground black pepper

Preheat the oven to 350°F.

Prick the pie crust with a fork and bake according to package directions. Remove from the oven and set aside to cool.

Fry the bacon in a large skillet over medium heat for about 8 minutes, until done but not crisp. Remove from the heat and transfer the bacon to a plate lined with paper towels to absorb any excess grease (reserve the bacon grease in the skillet). Chop the bacon into small pieces and set aside.

Return the skillet with the bacon grease to low heat. Add the butter and swirl until melted. Add the onions to the skillet, spreading them into a single layer if possible, and cook them slowly until they have begun to brown on the bottom. Stir until the onions are mostly turned over, allowing the other side to brown. Cook, continuing to stir the onions, until they are a caramel brown color, 30 to 45 minutes. Remove from the heat and drain off any excess fat. Add the sage and chopped bacon and set aside to cool to room temperature.

Beat the eggs in small bowl. Add the half-and-half and beat together. Season with the salt and black pepper.

Spoon the onion/bacon mixture into the pie shell. Pour the egg mixture over the onions and bacon, allowing it to soak into the crevices. Bake until the tart is set, 45 to 60 minutes. Remove from the oven and set aside for at least 5 minutes before serving. Garnish with more of the sage leaves, if desired, and serve.

NOTE: The tart can be made a day ahead, cooked, cooled, and then refrigerated. Reheat in a 350°F oven for 10 to 15 minutes.

Summer Squash Soup

The Anchorage, built in the early 1800s, is one of Beaufort's signature homes. By the 1930s it was being operated as a "guest home," what we'd now call a bed and breakfast, by the family of my grandmother's friend Dreka Stokes. When Mrs. Stokes sold it, it was converted into a restaurant, and one of the items on their menu was this wonderful cold squash soup. After being closed for many years, the Anchorage has now been returned to its former glory as an inn, and the restaurant has reopened as the Ribault Social Club. This soup is great in the summer for a cool treat served with a fruit salad and a sausage muffin; it's equally good served warm in the fall and winter.

Makes 4 servings

2 tablespoons unsalted butter

1 medium onion, chopped

1 pound yellow crookneck squash, sliced

1½ cups chicken stock (see note)

½ cup sour cream (see note), plus more for serving

½ teaspoon salt

¼ teaspoon white pepper

¼ teaspoon freshly grated nutmeg

Fresh dill for garnish

Melt the butter in a saucepan over medium heat and add the onion. Cook for 1 minute. Add the squash and chicken stock and cook for 10 to 15 minutes, until you can easily stick a fork through the squash. Remove from the heat, transfer to a blender, add the remaining ingredients, and blend well.

Chill for at least 2 hours or overnight before serving. Serve with a dollop of the sour cream and garnish with a sprinkling of the fresh dill.

NOTE: For a vegetarian version, substitute vegetable stock for chicken stock.

For a healthier version, substitute plain Greek yogurt for the sour cream.

Cheesy Pudding

This dish was one of Aunt Mimi's entertaining standbys—especially as a side with shrimp salad at luncheons. Once, I attended a cooking school in Columbia to learn how to make a very complicated crab and cheese soufflé. After holding our breath in hopes that the soufflé wouldn't fall, the group I was with bit into it with great anticipation. I must admit, I was a little unimpressed—for all the effort it took, I wouldn't have turned around for the difference between that fancy-schmancy soufflé and Aunt Mimi's cheesy pudding. Serve this plain as a side dish or add your choice of fillings to make it more of a main dish.

Makes 8 to 10 servings

12 slices white bread

5 tablespoons unsalted butter, at room temperature, plus more for greasing

2½ cups freshly grated extra sharp Cheddar

3 cups whole milk

4 whole large eggs

1 teaspoon salt

½ teaspoon dry mustard

Grease a 9 × 13-inch glass casserole dish with butter or butter-flavored baking spray.

Trim the crusts from the bread and spread the butter on each slice. Cut each slice into 4 square pieces. Alternate layers of the bread and the Cheddar in the prepared dish, with Cheddar as the final layer.

Whisk together the milk, eggs, salt, and dry mustard in a medium bowl and pour the mixture over the contents of the dish. Press down on the bread lightly with a fork, making sure each piece is covered by the milk mixture. Cover with plastic wrap and refrigerate overnight.

Preheat the oven to 350°F.

Bake for about 40 minutes. Remove from the oven and serve hot.

NOTE: In between the first and second layers of cheese and bread, add any number of fillings. Cooked bacon, sausage, diced ham, cooked shrimp, crab, or any combination thereof will work well.

Copper Carrot Pennies

My grandmother was a wonderful storyteller in the old-fashioned tradition. One of my favorite memories of spending the summers with her in Greer was our bedtime ritual of her telling me stories while rubbing my head to get me to fall asleep. Some of her favorites included *Goldilocks and the Three Bears, The Little Red Hen,* and *The Emperor's New Clothes.*

Each contained life lessons that have served me well over the years. From *Goldilocks,* I learned to not to be too picky and to not take things that didn't belong to me. From the *Little Red Hen,* I learned the importance of teamwork and always doing my fair share of the work if I wanted to enjoy the fruits of the labor. (If I heard, "Many hands make light work," once from my Gran-Gran, I heard it a thousand times.) And during my career in government and politics, I have run across many "emperors" and people of the court who didn't speak up because only the *smartest and best people* could see the emperor's fine new suit of clothes. We've all known someone who everyone just thought was the latest and greatest, and we wanted to be like the little boy in the story who screamed out, "He's *naked*—can't you just see he's *naked!*" But usually these folks, much like with the emperor in the story, get *exposed* in the end.

Gran-Gran continued her stories with the generation following mine, even after she moved to Beaufort. The father of one of my younger cousins was a health enthusiast *long* before it was popular, so whenever his son would come to visit, the little fellow was overjoyed: getting to have white bread was a real treat—not to mention all the sweets my mother and aunts would make for him. He also loved this carrot dish, so Gran-Gran always fixed it for him. My mother and aunts carried on this tradition when he was a cadet at The Citadel and would come down to visit them on nights when he could get a pass.

Makes 6 to 8 servings

2 pounds carrots, sliced

1 onion, sliced

1 green bell pepper, diced

1 (10½-ounce) can tomato soup

¾ cup granulated sugar or an equal amount of Splenda

¾ cup apple cider vinegar

2 tablespoons vegetable oil

1 tablespoon Worcestershire sauce

¾ teaspoon dry mustard

½ teaspoon salt

¼ teaspoon freshly ground black pepper or to taste

Fill a medium saucepan ¾ of the way full with water. Place it over medium heat and bring to a boil. Add the carrots and boil for about 10 minutes, until just tender. Remove from the heat and drain well. Transfer the carrots to a large bowl and add the onion and bell pepper.

Combine the remaining ingredients in a medium saucepan over medium heat and cook, stirring often, until the sugar has dissolved and the mixture is well blended. Remove from the heat. Pour the mixture over the carrots and refrigerate for at least 24 to 48 hours.

Serve cold.

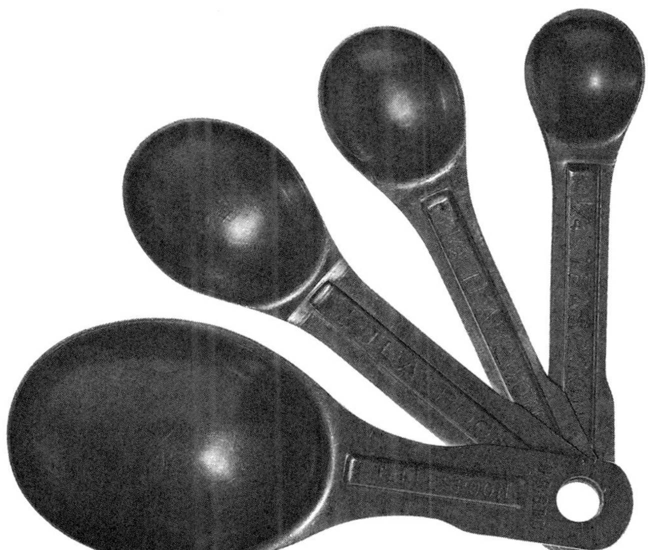

Mimi's Mac and Cheese

Once upon a time, in a land far, far away (let's call it Mississippi), there lived a fair matron who was the first lady of her town, the wife of the long-time mayor. We will call her Flora. Long after the mayor, who was known for his beautiful roses, had passed away, Flora did her best to continue to care for them. But Flora was thwarted at every turn by evil squirrels, who would eat the buds off the roses right in front of her big plate-glass window.

At dinner with friends one night, Flora lamented about the plight of the mayor's roses, and the host offered to show her his *squirrel swimming pool.* He took her to his back yard and there it was: an eighty-gallon trash-can filled with water. It was large enough for a squirrel trap to fit inside. Once trapped, the squirrels took a swim from which they did not return alive. Nothing else would do: Flora had to have a *squirrel swimming pool* all her own.

Several weeks later, Flora summoned her adult daughter to the home place, telling her she needed to talk to her because she was "the closest one." Now, for whatever reason, Dutiful Daughter (we will henceforth call her Deedee) took her mother's reference to her being the *closest one* to mean that she was the *closest to her heart.* She should have known that was not the case, especially since her older brother was clearly her mother's golden child. (He wasn't just the golden child; Deedee often joked that her brother possessed the golden *rod* as well, because he'd produced male heirs to carry on the family name.) Deedee just *knew* her mother was calling her, her *closest one,* to the homestead to discuss the rather large diamond ring her father had given her mother on the occasion of their fiftieth wedding anniversary.

Once Deedee arrived, her mother started talking about squirrel swimming pools. Deedee really had no idea what squirrel swimming pools had to do with her mother's diamond ring, but she went along, thinking this was just one of her mother's side-track conversations before they got down to the important stuff. Her mother explained everything about the squirrels' *swims* and that she'd been placing the recently departed squirrels in the trash, but that they began to smell before trash pick-up day.

"Put them in a plastic grocery bag, Mother," Deedee told her.

"I've been *double bagging* them," replied Flora, "and they still stink." At that point, Flora rose from the sofa.

"At last!" Deedee thought. *Finally,* they were headed to the jewelry box to have the big ring discussion. Instead, Flora headed in the opposite direction—toward the garage and the freezer there.

"I've been putting them in ziplock bags and putting them in the freezer. Since *you are the closest one* and will get here first if something happens to me, I need you to make sure they are all out of the freezer before the ladies from the Baptist church get here and need to put casseroles in there."

Deedee was stunned. When her mother had said, "*closest one,*" she had meant that Deedee lived in the closest proximity, geographically speaking, to her.

"But don't put them in the trash," Flora continued. "I've checked it out, and there's a dumpster behind Bubber's Liquor Store. Take them and put them there." Now Flora, being a good Baptist, had probably never been inside a liquor store in her life, but she'd taken a reconnaissance mission and cruised down the main drag in their small town to find a place to hide the evidence of her squirrel swimming pool.

So, daughters, if something happens to your mother and you are *the closest one,* be sure to do a quick check of the freezer before the ladies from the church start bringing those casseroles! And while you're at it, stir up this macaroni and cheese to have on hand, because you just know someone is going to bring a ham!

Make 8 to 10 servings

- 1 (16-ounce) box elbow macaroni
- 6 whole large eggs
- 1 quart whole milk
- 2 teaspoons salt
- 1 teaspoon dry mustard
- ¾ teaspoon freshly ground black pepper
- 1 pound extra sharp Cheddar, freshly grated
- 8 tablespoons (1 stick) unsalted butter
- 1 cup panko breadcrumbs

Preheat the oven to 350°F. Grease a 9 × 13-inch casserole dish with butter or cooking spray.

Cook the macaroni according to package directions, remove from the heat, and drain well.

In a medium bowl, beat the eggs. Add the milk, salt, dry mustard, and black pepper and mix well.

Place half the macaroni in the prepared dish and layer half the Cheddar over it. Repeat, reserving a little Cheddar for the top. Pour the egg mixture over the macaroni. Cut the butter into small pats and place them on top; cover with the reserved Cheddar.

Bake for 30 minutes. Remove from the oven and sprinkle the panko on top. Return to the oven and bake for 20 minutes more. Remove from the oven and serve hot.

Momma's Potato Salad

When I was in college, a friend invited me to come with him to his family's home in Pawleys Island, South Carolina, for a long weekend. My mother, who would never allow her Southern daughter to go somewhere empty-handed, made a *huge* bowl of potato salad. It must have been quite popular, as when I attended his mother's funeral some thirty-five years later, his older sister was still talking about how good that potato salad was.

These days, my friend lives in Atlanta, but he still goes to Pawleys with his family every summer. And what do you think he stops by my house in Columbia to pick up on his way to the beach? A big bowl of my version of my momma's potato salad.

Makes 10 to 12 servings

- 5 pounds Yukon Gold potatoes
- 3 teaspoons salt
- 6 hardboiled eggs, peeled and chopped
- 1 cup finely diced celery (about 3 stalks)
- ¾ cup finely diced onion
- ½ cup sweet pickle relish, drained
- 1 cup Duke's mayonnaise
- 3 tablespoons prepared yellow mustard
- 1 tablespoon apple cider vinegar
- 1 tablespoon granulated sugar
- 1 teaspoon freshly ground black pepper

Peel the potatoes and rinse off any remaining dirt under cold water. Cut the potatoes into ½-inch cubes. Place them in a large pot and cover with cold water. Add 1 teaspoon of the salt, place the pot over medium heat, and bring to a boil. Reduce the heat to low and cook for 10 to 15 minutes, until a fork can be easily stuck into the potatoes (do not overcook the potatoes). Remove from the heat and drain well.

Transfer the potatoes to a large bowl and set aside to cool (place in the refrigerator to speed the cooling process if necessary).

Once the potatoes are cool, add the eggs, celery, onion, and relish to the bowl and mix well.

In a separate bowl, mix together the mayonnaise, the mustard, the vinegar, the sugar, the remaining 2 teaspoons salt, and the black pepper. Add the mayonnaise mixture to the potato mixture and mix well. Refrigerate for several hours to allow the flavors to develop.

Serve cold.

CHEATER'S POTATO SALAD

If you are pinched for time, here's an easy way to make a store-bought potato salad something special. To a 4-pound container of red-skinned potato salad, add 1 cup bacon bits, 1 cup freshly grated sharp Cheddar or crumbled blue cheese, and ½ to 1 teaspoon freshly ground black pepper. Mix well and transfer to a beautiful serving bowl. Rinse out the potato salad container and hide it in the recycling bin.

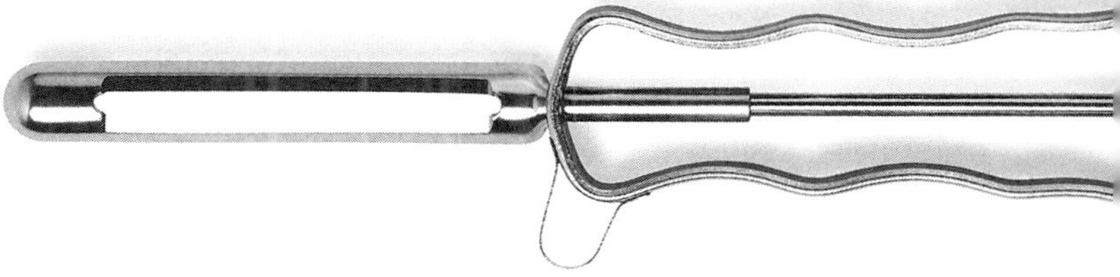

Easy Fried Okra

Okra is one of those quintessential Southern dishes that everyone loves or hates—there is usually very little middle ground. This is my best friend Jane's method for cooking okra, and I'll bet that you'll find it can turn most anyone into an okra fan. Using seafood breading with the seasoning already included makes it extra easy. If I'm serving this as an appetizer, I cut the tops off the okra, fry the pods whole, and serve them with Alabama White Sauce for dipping. Try to find pods that are no longer than 3 to 4 inches in length (about the size of your little finger) for this version.

If I'm serving this dish as a green vegetable with dinner, usually alongside crab cakes, red rice, and creamed corn, I'll cut it crosswise in ½ inch pieces. Either way, you'll be craving more, so always cook more than you think you will need!

Makes 3 to 4 servings

1 pound fresh okra

2 whole large eggs

2 tablespoons water

2 cups seasoned seafood breading mix, such as House Autry brand

Vegetable oil for frying

Alabama White Sauce for serving (recipe follows)

Wash the okra in a colander and shake well to remove any excess water. Set aside to dry on a plate lined with paper towels if desired.

Beat together the eggs and water in a large bowl. Add the okra to the bowl and toss until the okra is well coated. Place the okra in a large ziplock bag or a medium paper bag and add the seafood breading mix. Shake well until the okra is fully coated with the breading.

Add ¾ of an inch of the oil to a skillet (preferably cast iron) and heat the oil to 350°F. Sift the okra through your fingers while still in the bag to let any excess breading fall away and add it in small batches to the hot oil. Fry for 5 to 6 minutes, turning occasionally so the okra browns evenly. Transfer the fried okra to a platter lined with paper towels to absorb any grease and keep the platter in a warm oven. (This is important for two reasons: 1. it will keep it warm, and 2. it will keep it from all getting eaten before the rest of it is fried.) Repeat until all the okra has been fried. Remove from the oven and serve warm.

NOTE: Here's a tip from my eldest goddaughter Windy: if you'd like to make it a little spicier, add 1 teaspoon of Old Bay seasoning to the seafood breading.

ALABAMA WHITE SAUCE

This is an excellent dipping sauce for the okra pods.

Makes 1½ cups

- 1 cup Duke's mayonnaise or Miracle Whip salad dressing
- ¼ cup apple cider vinegar
- 1 tablespoon Creole or Dijon-style mustard
- 1 tablespoon prepared horse-radish
- 1 tablespoon freshly squeezed lemon juice
- ½ teaspoon minced garlic
- ¼ teaspoon ground cayenne pepper
- ¼ teaspoon smoked paprika
- ¼ teaspoon salt

Combine all of the ingredients in a blender and pulse until well blended. Store in a 1-quart jar in the refrigerator and use as needed; it is excellent as a dip or spread on boneless chicken breasts before grilling.

Pineapple au Gratin

The first time I remember having this dish was at the repast after my grandmother's funeral in 1992. My Gran-Gran lived to be a hundred years old, and I can't imagine what my life would have been like without her being part of it. My eldest goddaughter Windy was born the December before Gran-Gran died. I couldn't conceive of a life without Gran-Gran, but when Windy came along, it was like Gran-Gran said to me, "You've got a new little person to love now and to be in your life. I'm tired, and I'm going home."

My grandmother was a lifelong devotee of *As the World Turns (ATWT)*. You did not talk to or call my grandmother while *ATWT* was on—an honor she also bestowed on Lawrence Welk and Walter Cronkite. After Gran-Gran retired from teaching, she and my aunts all lived together in the house in Beaufort. Each night at dinner, she'd fill them in on all the details of the happenings in Oakdale, the fictional town where *ATWT* was set.

One night, when Mimi asked what happened on *ATWT* that day, Gran-Gran said she hadn't watched it. Mimi and Mary Dob were stunned but didn't say anything. This went on for about two weeks, so, finally, they asked my grandmother if something was wrong. After some hemming and hawing, Gran-Gran finally 'fessed up that when she was saying her prayers one night, praying for all her children, grandchildren, family, and friends, she'd also prayed that Lisa, the resident hussy on *ATWT,* would be kinder to Bob, her long-suffering doctor husband. Gran-Gran told my aunts that she'd realized that if she was praying for people who didn't exist, then perhaps watching her *stories,* as she referred to her soaps, was getting a little out of hand.

Mimi and Mary Dob assured her they thought it would be okay, and shortly thereafter, she went back to watching *ATWT* every day until she passed away. I don't think she ever forgave Richard Nixon for Watergate—not because of the crimes his administration committed, but because the hearings pre-empted *As the World Turns* for weeks on end.

Every time I make this recipe, I think of my grandmother—and of Lisa and Bob! My Gran-Gran had a heart so loving that she even prayed for people who didn't really exist!

Makes 8 servings

- ½ to 1 cup granulated sugar
- ¼ cup + 2 tablespoons all-purpose flour
- 2 (20-ounce) cans pineapple chunks in juice (not syrup)
- 2 cups freshly grated extra sharp Cheddar
- 1½ sleeves butter-flavored crackers, crumbled
- 8 tablespoons (1 stick) unsalted butter, melted

Preheat the oven to 375°F. Grease a 2-quart casserole dish with butter or cooking spray.

In a large bowl, stir together the sugar and flour. Add the pineapple and stir until just blended.

Transfer the contents of the bowl into the prepared casserole dish. Sprinkle the Cheddar over the top.

In a medium bowl, combine the crumbled crackers and melted butter. Sprinkle the contents of the bowl over the Cheddar. Bake for 20 to 30 minutes. Remove from the oven.

Serve hot.

Sarah Seabrook's Red Rice

Left, Odessa "Dessie" (née Cabbagestalk) Williams Jenkins, and right, Sarah Seabrook, Easter Sunday, 1964.

Sarah Seabrook, the red rice queen of Beaufort, worked for many years for the late Mayor Henry C. Chambers and was a very important part of his family. Sarah shared her talent for making red rice with many people in the community—especially at the fried chicken suppers held at her church, the Grace African Methodist Episcopal (AME) Church on Charles Street.

Sarah's original recipe called for a large can of tomatoes. Everyone else in Beaufort loved Sarah's red rice just the way it was, but one of the few failures of my Lowcountry upbringing is my inability to find big, squishy chunks of tomatoes appetizing. So, I have adapted Sarah's recipe, and I use tomato paste. I think it's pretty terrific; when I shared it once with a Beaufort friend who had grown up in Charleston, it brought tears to his eyes. He told me it was just like his mother's, and that's close enough for me. I think Sarah would be pleased that her name and tradition are still carried on and loved.

Makes 8 servings

8 strips bacon

2 medium onions, finely chopped

1 green or red bell pepper, chopped

1 tablespoon minced garlic

1½ cups water (see notes)

1 (6-ounce) can tomato paste

2 teaspoons salt

2 teaspoons granulated sugar

2 teaspoons Old Bay seasoning

2 cups uncooked white rice

Fry the bacon in a large skillet over medium heat for about 8 minutes, until done but not crisp. Remove from the heat and transfer the bacon to a plate lined with paper towels to absorb any excess grease (reserve the bacon grease in the skillet). Chop the bacon into small pieces and set aside.

Add the onions, pepper, and garlic to the skillet. Return it to medium heat and cook for about 5 minutes, until the onions are translucent and the chopped pepper is tender. Add the water, tomato paste, salt, sugar, and Old Bay seasoning and stir to combine. Reduce the heat to low and simmer for 10 minutes until mixture has thickened slightly. Add the rice to the tomato mixture and stir until the rice is well coated. Add bacon and stir well.

Transfer the rice to the top of a rice steamer and steam for about 1 to 1½ hours, until the rice is done and fluffs easily with a fork. If you don't have a rice steamer, pour the mixture into a greased 3-quart round covered casserole and bake in a 350°F oven for 1 hour, stirring occasionally to fluff the rice.

Remove from the steamer or oven and serve hot.

NOTES: You can use the tomato paste can to measure out the water—just refill it twice. This also helps get all of the tomato paste out of the can.

Red rice can be easily reheated in the microwave if made in advance or if you are reheating it for a midnight snack. Add a little water to the rice, cover with plastic wrap and heat.

If you want this dish to be more like a jambalaya, add one pound of chopped kielbasa sausage when frying the bacon. When the rice is almost through steaming, just before serving, add 1 pound raw, peeled and deveined small to medium shrimp to the top of the steamer and steam for about 5 minutes. Be sure to let the shrimp steam until they are pink, but do not overcook them. Turn out the red rice and shrimp into a large serving bowl and mix well before serving.

Summer Corn

Dempsey Farms has been located on St. Helena Island for the past sixty years; today, a fourth generation of family members works the farm. Their season begins with strawberries in the spring; okra, tomatoes, squash, and peppers in the summer; and pumpkins in the fall. But to me, the best crop of all is their corn—white "Milky Way," or bicolored, it doesn't matter one bit. It's all wonderful.

Putting up (as we always referred to it) summer corn has been a tradition in my family for as long as I can remember. Once I was older, I was assigned to cut the corn off the cobs. We used a great device from the Lee Manufacturing Company: a stainless steel tool about eighteen inches long that had a well in the middle of the metal and a blade about halfway up the well. My job was to slide the corn along the well, and the blade removed the corn from the cobs. A grater on the other side of the blade scraped the cobs to get any remaining corn and juice. If you're planning to process corn on an ongoing basis, it's well worth the price! You can find them at our beloved GrayCo Hardware in Beaufort, at the Mast General Store, or online.

Makes 3 quarts

30 ears corn

¼ cup corn oil

1 cup whole milk or half-and-half

Shuck the corn ears by removing all green husks and scraping away the corn silks with a vegetable brush (holding the cobs under running water makes silking easier).

Cut the corn from the cobs either by investing in the corn cutter and creamer I mentioned above, or place each cob upright in the middle of a tube or Bundt pan and cut along the sides of the cob, allowing the corn to fall into the pan. Scrape the knife along the edge of the cob to get any remaining kernels and "milk" the corn.

Place the corn oil in the bottom of a heavy stockpot and swirl until the bottom is fully coated. Add the corn and milk, place over medium-to-low heat, and bring to a slow boil (watch it carefully so the corn does not burn or scorch).

Once the corn begins to boil, reduce the heat to low and cook for 15 minutes. Remove from the heat and set aside to cool. Freeze the corn in 1-quart containers and use it for Corn and Crab Chowder (see recipe on (p. 107) or prepare it as creamed corn.

CREAMED CORN

Makes 4 servings

- 1 quart corn as prepared above, fresh or frozen and thawed (or about 10 ears)
- ½ cup half-and-half
- 6 tablespoons unsalted butter
- ½ to ¾ teaspoon salt
- ½ teaspoon freshly ground black pepper or to taste

Place the corn in a heavy saucepan over low-to-medium heat. Add the half-and-half and butter and cook uncovered, until thickened and any liquid is cooked off. Add seasonings to taste. Stir well and remove from the heat. Serve hot.

Baked Potato Casserole

For many summers, we joined friends on a mountain weekend trip to Highlands and Cashiers, North Carolina. Everyone who went along loved to cook, and each of us cooked special dishes during the weekend. One of the guys who enjoyed making omelets would cook them made-to-order for breakfast with all the accoutrements—several kinds of cheese, bacon, onions, green onions, and so on. On the last night of each trip, another of the guys would always cook ribeye steaks on the grill. To go with them, I'd make my brother George's twice-baked potatoes with the leftover omelet ingredients so we didn't have to tote them home or toss them out.

This casserole is an easier version of twice-baked potatoes. If you want to serve the potatoes in their skins, after baking them, cut off the top third of each potato and carefully scoop the flesh away from the skin, leaving at least ¼ inch of potato flesh all around. Mix the ingredients together and stuff the mixture into the reserved potato skins. Bake the stuffed potatoes until they are heated all the way through, 15 to 20 minutes.

If you make this casserole and have leftovers, add a little whole milk and turn it into a great potato soup. Just place a scoop of the leftovers in a microwave-safe bowl, add a little milk, and stir until it is the consistency of a thick soup. Cook it in the microwave on high for 2 to 3 minutes. Serve topped with a little cheese and some crumbled bacon.

Makes 10 to 12 servings

- 10 large russet potatoes (about 7 pounds)
- 9 tablespoons unsalted butter
- 1 cup sour cream
- ½ cup heavy cream
- 1 to 1½ teaspoons salt
- 1½ teaspoons freshly ground black pepper
- 3 cups freshly grated mild Cheddar
- 1 pound bacon, cooked until crisp and crumbled
- 3 cups freshly grated extra sharp white Cheddar
- 3 whole large eggs, lightly beaten
- ½ cup finely chopped green onion

Preheat the oven to 400°F.

Wash and scrub the potatoes. Place them on a baking sheet and bake until a fork can easily be inserted into the centers, about 1 hour and 15 minutes. Remove from the oven and set aside to cool until they can be comfortably handled.

Reduce the oven temperature to 375°F. Grease a 9 × 13-inch baking dish with 1 tablespoon butter.

Cut the potatoes in half and scoop out the flesh into a large bowl. Add the sour cream, the remaining 8 tablespoons butter, the heavy cream, the salt, and the black pepper and mash with a potato masher or hand mixer until well blended. Add the bacon, the mild Cheddar, 2 cups of the white Cheddar, the eggs, and the green onion and mix thoroughly.

Transfer the potato mixture to the prepared dish and top with the remaining 1 cup white Cheddar. The casserole can be made a day ahead, covered, and placed in the refrigerator. If made ahead, remove the cover and allow the casserole to come to room temperature before baking.

Bake until the mixture is light golden brown and all the cheese is melted, 35 to 40 minutes. Remove from the oven and set aside to cool for 5 to 10 minutes before serving. Serve warm.

Champagne Mustard

This mustard is the basis for so many things I love to cook—deviled eggs and salad dressing, to name a couple—and it makes a wonderful sauce for chicken. I once gave a jar of it to a friend who was a businessman in downtown Columbia. His wife later told me that he stopped scheduling lunches out because he loved this mustard so much, he wanted an excuse to bring a sandwich.

It's also a perfect Christmas gift or hostess present. Design your own jar label using a template provided with a package of labels and then follow the directions on the package to print them out on your home printer.

Champagne vinegar can be found in the condiment section of most grocery or gourmet stores. To make your own, pour a bottle of inexpensive (or leftover) champagne into a wide-mouthed glass jar, cover with several layers of cheesecloth to prevent bugs or dust from getting in, and secure the top with a piece of twine or ribbon. Set aside in a cool, dry place for at least one month or as long as three months; taste it periodically to determine if it has turned to vinegar. Once it turns, decant it into a bottle (screw-top wine bottles are great for this purpose) and store it in the pantry.

Makes 4 cups

4 whole large eggs

1 cup granulated sugar

½ cup dry mustard

½ cup Champagne or Prosecco vinegar

¼ cup sherry

Place all of the ingredients in a blender and blend on high speed for 5 minutes. Transfer the contents of the blender to a glass double boiler or a heatproof glass bowl placed on top of a metal saucepan (the mustard and vinegar cannot come into contact with any kind of metal after they are mixed together). Cook, stirring occasionally, for about 20 to 25 minutes, until thickened. Use with meats, on sandwiches, in salads, and in deviled eggs. Keep refrigerated.

CHAMPAGNE MUSTARD SALAD DRESSING

One of my mother's dearest friends passed away at a time when my mother and Aunt Mimi had their hands full taking care of my Aunt Mary. I had been very close to my mother's friend and to her children, all of whom were older than me and had been very kind to George and me during our childhood, so I offered to cook a meal for the family the night before the funeral. I made a big batch of crab cakes, two pots of red rice, and a long lemon pound cake. I brought it all with me to Beaufort and first stopped by the house to pick up Mother and Aunt Mimi for our visit with the family. My mother surveyed all the food I had cooked, and instead of saying, "Oh, sweetie, thank you for doing all this," she instead said, "You didn't make them a green vegetable?"

Now, I probably could have argued that the red rice had green pepper in it, but I was so taken aback that I grabbed the keys off the counter and headed to the grocery store. I threw together a mixed green salad and bought some dressing to go with it.

The next week, I came up with this as my signature vinaigrette. It's now the house dressing at my home, and I try not to ever be without a bottle of it in the refrigerator— just in case I need to whip up a green vegetable!

Makes 3½ cups

- 1 cup balsamic vinegar (try pear or fig flavored)
- ½ cup Champagne Mustard or Dijon-style mustard
- ¼ cup packed light brown sugar
- 1 cup extra virgin olive oil
- 1 cup vegetable oil

Place all of the ingredients in a blender and blend on high speed. Transfer to a 1-quart Mason jar or a wine bottle with a screw top and store in the refrigerator. Shake well before using if it has been stored. Serve over mixed greens with goat cheese, Craisins, candied walnuts, and bacon bits.

Tidalholm Salad Dressing

The Tidalholm is a beautiful nineteenth-century home built by the Fripp family in a historic area of downtown Beaufort known as "the Point." For many years, it was operated as a "guest home," a forerunner to present-day bed-and-breakfasts. It attracted artists, authors, professors, and statesmen to Beaufort, where they could enjoy our mild winters. This recipe for the house dressing at Tidalholm was given to my mother by the lady who catered many of their events.

You say you've never heard of the Tidalholm? Maybe you know it by its modern-day nickname—*The Big Chill* house. The movie was filmed there in 1983, as well as the movie adaptation of *The Great Santini,* a novel by Beaufort's favorite son Pat Conroy, filmed in 1979. It's been voted the most famous house in South Carolina.

Makes 2½ cups

½ cup granulated sugar

½ cup apple cider vinegar

½ cup extra virgin olive oil

½ cup canola or sunflower oil

½ cup ketchup

1 teaspoon Worcestershire sauce

1 tablespoon finely grated onion (can use a Vidalia)

2 tablespoons celery seed

1 teaspoon salt

¼ teaspoon garlic powder

⅛ teaspoon smoked paprika (optional)

⅛ teaspoon cayenne pepper

In a saucepan over medium heat, stir the vinegar and sugar together until the sugar dissolves. Remove from the heat and set aside to cool.

Combine the remaining ingredients in a blender. Add the vinegar mixture and pulse until well blended. Transfer to a glass jar or other airtight container for storage; it will keep refrigerated for several weeks.

NOTE: This is also great as a dressing for coleslaw or a marinade for grilled meat or chicken.

4

Meats and Poultry

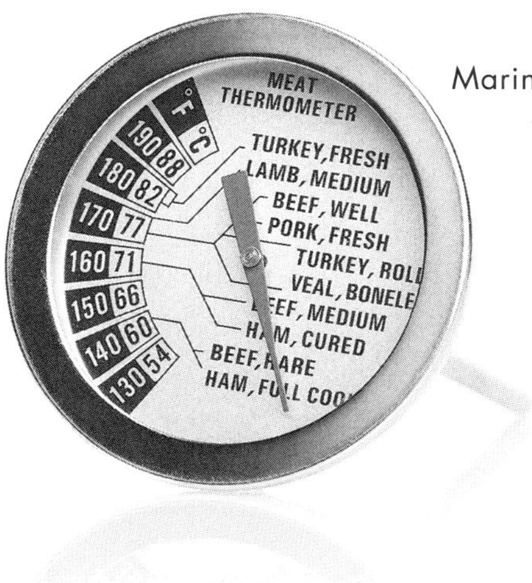

The Social Pig

The Devine Street Piggly Wiggly in Columbia has long been known as "The Social Pig." They even sell T-shirts with that moniker emblazoned on the back. For many years it has been situated at the intersection of Shandon and Heathwood—two of the most hoity-toity neighborhoods of Columbia. Back when upper- and middle-class women typically didn't work, it was the gathering place for matrons when they weren't at the bridge table, garden club, or Junior League. They would shop the aisles in their shirtwaist dresses, pumps, and pearls and catch up on all the neighborhood gossip.

"Oh, dahling, what a cute, cute frock that is!"

"Why, how are those *preeeecious* grandchildren of yours?"

"How's Bootie doing—has he passed that gallstone yet?"

Everything you needed to know about the neighborhood could be found out between the Social Pig and the Winn-Dixie. Over time, as women have taken our place in the workforce, the true societal nature of the Social Pig has waned. But you still run into the collective mavens of Shandon and Heathwood there every now and then. There's a completely inverse relationship between how well-coiffed and dressed you are and how many people you will run into at the Social Pig. Stop by after work with perfect hair, full makeup, and a business suit, and you won't run into a soul you know. Slump in on the way home from the gym, all nasty with sweaty hair pulled back into a ponytail, and you'll run into every person you know or have ever thought about knowing! It's a fact of life at the Social Pig, and it almost never fails. (Sadly, at the time of publication of this book, the Social Pig is being threatened with possible takeover by a Lidl!)

Jane's Slow Cooker Pulled Pork

South Carolina is known for its barbeque, which almost always involves a pig. You can tell when someone has moved here from "off" when they refer to cooking hamburgers and hot dogs on a grill as barbequing or having a barbeque. Oh, honey, no. That is merely "cooking out." A barbeque involves a pig cooked over coals low and slow for many hours while imbibing in little brown beverages. (Preferably the pig has previously been marinated in a bathtub overnight and has scared the hell out of at least one bleary-eyed person who only woke up to stumble into the bathroom for relief.)

This is a *much* easier version of pulled pork barbeque. I like to start mine out in the smoker for a couple of hours and then finish it off in the slow cooker when the temperature of the meat begins to stall in the smoker. You could do the same thing on the grill with some wood chips added to the coals. It's equally good cooked completely in the slow cooker with the Mustard BBQ Sauce below or up to 3 cups of the barbeque sauce of your choice.

Makes 10 to 12 servings

PULLED PORK

1 (5- to 7-pound) pork butt

Extra virgin olive oil

½ cup commercial pork butt dry rub

1 cup apple cider vinegar

3 to 4 sprigs fresh rosemary

MUSTARD BBQ SAUCE

1 cup prepared yellow mustard

1 cup ketchup

½ cup Duke's mayonnaise

½ cup apple cider vinegar

½ cup packed dark brown sugar

¼ cup soy or Worcestershire sauce

Several dashes hot sauce

Make the Pulled Pork: Rub the pork butt with the oil and liberally apply the pork butt dry rub.

Warm a heavy skillet over medium-high heat. Sear the pork butt in the skillet, turning it over several times, about 3 to 4 minutes on each side, until a good crust forms.

Pour the vinegar into a large slow cooker. Add the pork butt and place the rosemary sprigs on top. Cover and cook on low for 6 to 8 hours, until the meat falls apart when pulled with a fork. Remove from the slow cooker, reserving the cooking liquid, and set aside to cool for 1 hour.

Make the Mustard BBQ Sauce: Combine all of the ingredients in a blender and pulse until fully combined.

Shred the pork with a knife and fork. Mix as much of the Mustard BBQ Sauce as you like with the pulled pork until it is coated to your preference. Add a little of the cooking liquid and some extra pork butt dry rub to add extra flavor to your barbeque and achieve the preferred taste and consistency of the sauce.

Store any of the remaining Mustard BBQ Sauce in the refrigerator.

Beef and Sour Cream

This recipe was a staple in my family, enjoyed by several generations and one of the first meals I learned to cook on my own. My grandmother's church in Greer published a cookbook when I was in the seventh grade, and this recipe was in it. I've been cooking it ever since! When my cousin Scoot was at The Citadel, he requested this dish every time he came down to Beaufort to visit my mother and aunts on an evening pass. Serve it over white rice instead of noodles to make a Southern version of beef Stroganoff.

Makes 4 servings

1½ pounds round steak

¼ cup all-purpose flour

4 tablespoons unsalted butter

1 (13.5-ounce) can sliced mushrooms, drained

1 (10½-ounce) can beef consommé

1 (2-ounce) package dry onion soup mix

1 (8-ounce) container sour cream

Cooked rice or egg noodles for serving

Preheat the oven to 350°F. Grease a 2-quart casserole dish with cooking spray.

Cut the steak into bite-size pieces. Coat the steak in the flour.

Melt the butter in a skillet over medium heat. Add the steak pieces and cook until lightly browned.

Transfer the steak to the prepared casserole dish and add the mushrooms. Pour the consommé and soup mix over the steak and stir until combined.

Bake for 30 minutes. Remove from the oven and stir in the sour cream. Bake for 30 minutes more. Remove from the oven and serve over the rice or egg noodles.

NOTE: This can also be served as an appetizer in a chafing dish with toothpicks. Use beef tips cut into bite-size pieces and large button mushrooms. Omit the rice.

Chicken and White Bean Chili

This is the perfect easy entertaining dish for watching the big game or any other large gathering. The chili can be prepared ahead and reheated. Keep the pot warm on the stove or in a slow cooker and set up a chili buffet on the counter with all the condiments listed below. Serve with a big basket of homemade cornbread and a chopped salad mix. If there are leftovers, freeze them in individual containers that you can thaw and reheat in the microwave for a quick meal.

Makes 10 to 12 servings

- 1 pound dried Great Northern beans
- 6 cups chicken broth plus more as needed
- 2 medium onions, chopped
- 2 teaspoons minced garlic
- 1 tablespoon extra-virgin olive oil
- 2 (4-ounce) cans chopped green chiles
- 2 teaspoons ground cumin
- 1½ teaspoons dried oregano
- ¼ teaspoon ground cloves
- ¼ teaspoon ground cayenne pepper
- 4 cups shredded cooked chicken (see note)
- Choice of freshly grated Monterey Jack or Mexican blend cheese, sour cream or plain Greek yogurt, guacamole, chopped green onions, crushed tortilla chips, and/or salsa for topping

In a large stockpot over medium heat, combine the beans, the chicken broth, half the onions, and the garlic and bring to a boil. Reduce the heat to low and simmer for 3 hours or more, until the beans are very soft. Add more broth if necessary.

In a small skillet over medium heat, warm the oil. Add the remaining onion and cook until tender. Add the chiles and seasonings and stir until well combined. Cook for 2 to 3 minutes. Remove from the heat and add the contents of the skillet to the stockpot. Stir well. Add the chicken and continue to simmer for 1 hour. Remove from the heat.

Serve hot in bowls topped with your choice of toppings.

NOTE: Some club warehouse stores sell preshredded rotisserie chicken, making this easy dish even easier.

Cooper's Brisket

I am not a good griller. I want to slap the meat on the grill and let it cook; go inside and make the other fourteen sides to go with it; and come back and find the meat done so everything is magically ready at the same time. Grilling doesn't work that way.

However, several years ago I bought a smoker, which you can, in fact, put the meat in, walk away, and come back later to find it magically (mostly) ready. My friend Dan Cooper gave me this recipe for brisket, and it's been a winner for me and everyone else with whom I've shared it. I love it because you can put it in the smoker, get a good bit of smoke going, go to bed, let it cook overnight, and in the morning, it's all ready. (Since I still don't know how to grill, the grilling instructions below are from Coop.)

It's appropriate that this recipe involves smoke and fire, because one of the legendary Cooper stories from the State House involved his two-year battle with then-Governor Mark "Hike the Appalachian Trail" Sanford over a fire truck for Cooper's district. Cooper, the chairman of the House Ways and Means Committee, included funding for a ladder fire truck in the budget for his district. Governor Sanford went on a tear about "pork barrel" projects in the budget, going so far as to bring two piglets named "Pork" and "Barrel" to the second floor of the State House during the waning days of the legislative session to "highlight" his cause. The "highlights" turned into "lowlights" when the pigs defecated all over the governor's blazer, pants, and shoes, as well as the carpet of the recently renovated State House. The General Assembly found the whole thing to be extremely disrespectful both to the institution of the legislative branch and to the stature of the State House, and it greatly damaged the already rocky relationship between the governor and the legislature.

Meanwhile, back in the budget: Cooper's fire truck was safely tucked away—or so he thought. Sanford couldn't use his line-item veto to get to the fire truck because neither he nor anyone on his staff could *find* it. So instead, the governor attempted to create a whole new category of veto by describing it in his veto message under the title of "fiscal gimmickry." The House didn't buy *his* gimmickry and promptly overrode that veto. Once again, the fire truck was safe—*until* the governor threatened to fire the head of the agency whose budget contained the funding for the fire truck if he wrote the check for it. Cooper, being a good person, didn't want that to happen, so he relented and there was no fire truck—at least not yet.

The next year, Cooper put the fire truck in the budget of a Constitutional officer—someone the governor couldn't threaten—in another line that the governor couldn't find to veto. In the end, Cooper got his shiny new fire truck, which saved lives in an apartment fire in his district less than a year later. Governor Sanford went on to infamy for hiking the Appalachian Trail—or not—and later confessed to Joe Scarborough on MSNBC that "Pork" and "Barrel" ended up getting barbequed later that summer.

Makes 8 to 10 servings

- 1 (7-pound) beef brisket (see note)
- 1 cup commercial brisket rub
- 1 to 2 (12-ounce) cans light beer of choice

Place the brisket fat side up in a single-use aluminum pan. Rub it liberally with the brisket rub and set aside to come to room temperature, for an hour.

Smoking instructions: Preheat the smoker to 225°F. Pour 1 can of the beer into the aluminum pan and place the pan in the smoker. Smoke for 11 to 12 hours, checking to see if the second can of beer is needed around the 6-hour mark to keep the brisket from drying out, until the brisket is done and its internal temperature reaches 185°F.

Grilling instructions: You can cook the brisket on a grill over low heat for 12 hours, but you must tend to it regularly. On a gas grill, use wood chips soaked in water and wrapped in foil to achieve the smoke; you will need to replace the wood chips every few hours. On a charcoal grill, start with about 25 to 30 briquettes spread over the base. If you are able to hold your hand over the grill surface for 10–15 seconds to test the heat, the temperature is around 200°F to 250°F. Place pan containing the brisket on the grill, add beer, and close top of grill. Add between 15 to 25 briquettes every 2 to 3 hours to maintain that temperature. You may want to invest in a charcoal chimney if you choose this method.

Slow cooker instructions: If you don't have a smoker and don't want the labor associated with gas or charcoal grills, place the rubbed brisket in a slow cooker, pour 1 can of the beer over it, and cook on low for 8 hours, until the brisket is done and its internal temperature reaches 185°F.

NOTE: Make sure you buy a beef brisket, not a corned beef brisket. Depending on the crowd, a whole brisket will feed 15 to 20 people, so either cut it in half or ask the butcher to do it for you at the meat counter. Make sure to request the flat part if you do.

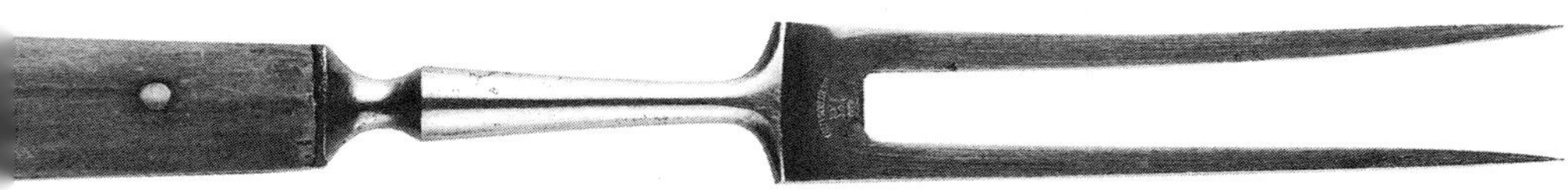

Slow Cooker Roast

According to the *Beaufort Gazette,* at 6:00 p.m. on Saturday, November 8, 1969, Mrs. Howard Danner of 411 Craven Street, known in Beaufort as "The Castle," opened her oven door to remove the roast her cook had placed there earlier in the day. The oven was empty, and the roast was gone. Mrs. Danner had just driven her cook home, and while she did, she left the house unlocked for a very short period of time. According to the report made by Beaufort City Police Officer G. D. Smith, "Either a very hungry person entered the house while Mrs. Danner was gone, or it may be surmised the 'Ghost of the Danner House' became hungry and absconded with the practically cooked roast, being unable to withstand the temptation of waiting for it to cook."

The Castle dates back to 1859, and according to legend, it is haunted by the ghost of a jester who sailed to the New World in 1563 with Beaufort's founder, the Frenchman Jean Ribault. As the story goes, the jester drowned in the Beaufort River. His ghost lived in the marsh beside the house and took up residence in the house when it was built, supposedly because it reminded him of his home in France. The ghost, named Gauche, has appeared to generations of the Johnson and Danner families, including the Mrs. Danner of this story, as well as to others who have occupied the house.

Serve the roast hot with the gravy, if using. Let this roast cook low and slow for 8 to 10 hours—hopefully, you and the ghost will be able to resist temptation of digging in before it's done.

Makes 6 to 8 servings

1 (3- to-5-pound) chuck roast

12 small red potatoes (optional)

4 carrots, peeled and cut into 3-inch pieces (optional)

1 (1-ounce) packet dry ranch seasoning mix

1 to 2 (1-ounce) packets au jus gravy mix

8 tablespoons (1 stick) unsalted butter

Grease the inside of a slow cooker with cooking spray. Place the chuck roast and the potatoes and carrots, if using, in the slow cooker and sprinkle the dry ranch seasoning mix and 1 packet of the au jus gravy mix on top of it. Place the butter on top and cook on low for 8 to 10 hours or on high for 4 to 7 hours. Transfer the roast and vegetables (if using) to a serving platter.

If desired, strain the cooking liquid into a large skillet. Add the remaining packet of au jus gravy mix if there is not enough gravy as is. Place the skillet over medium heat and bring to a boil. Reduce the heat to low and simmer for 5 minutes. Remove from the heat.

Hot Dog Chili

Johnnie Neville, my dear friend Mary Jo's dad, was one of fifteen children in a large Catholic family in Baltimore, Maryland. He spent three years in Europe in the Army Air Corps during World War II—tough duty by anyone's estimation. He returned home on a ship to Newport News, Virginia, and then caught a train home to Baltimore. The train pulled into Camden Yards, which was still a railroad yard then and not the beautiful baseball stadium it is today.

Johnnie's father worked at the B & O Railroad office, just up the street from Camden Yards. On the day he returned home, while Johnnie was making his way across the rail yard to find his father, he came upon a hot dog vendor whose dogs were legendary. Since Johnnie hadn't eaten a hot dog in three years, he ate one. In fact, it was so good that he ate another.

When he finally found his dad, he shared how good the hot dogs were and how much he had missed them while he was away fighting in the war—to which his devout Catholic father replied, "Son, it's Friday. You're not supposed to be eating meat!" I am quite sure that when Johnnie Neville met St. Peter at the Pearly Gates, the sin of eating two hot dogs on a Friday after coming home from the war was *not* listed in his book.

It has been lost to history as to whether Mr. Neville's hot dog included chili, but this is one of my favorite recipes and is a must at my cookouts.

Makes 24 toppings for dogs

- 1 pound ground beef (I use extra lean)
- 1 medium onion, chopped
- 1 cup ketchup
- 1 cup water
- 1 tablespoon prepared yellow mustard or Champagne Mustard (p. 78)
- 1 teaspoon salt
- ¼ teaspoon each freshly ground black pepper and ground cayenne pepper

In a skillet over low heat, cook the ground beef and onion until browned. Remove from the heat and transfer the mixture to a plate lined with paper towels to remove grease and pat the top with a paper towel to remove additional grease. Drain all remaining grease from the skillet.

Return the mixture to the skillet and add the remaining ingredients. Place the skillet over low heat and cook for 45 minutes. Remove from the heat and serve as a topping on hot dogs or nachos.

Key Lime Chicken Strips

This recipe originally was given to my mother by her dear friend Betty Waskiewicz, who found it in a cookbook from a bed and breakfast in Union, South Carolina. Miss Betty served this dish at the Valentine Ball Dinner in Beaufort one year, and I decided that it's the perfect chicken dish for tailgating or picnicking. Purchasing fresh garlic and ginger that is already minced, available in the produce section of the grocery store, makes them easy to prepare.

The strips can be fried the day before and placed in the refrigerator. On the day you want to serve them, pour the marinade mixture over the chicken and bake according to the directions. Wrap them up in foil and head to the game.

Makes 8 servings

½ cup Key lime juice*

1 teaspoon minced garlic

1 teaspoon minced ginger

16 chicken tenderloins

1 cup all-purpose flour

1 teaspoon garlic powder (not garlic salt)

1 teaspoon ground ginger

½ teaspoon salt

¼ teaspoon freshly ground black pepper

Canola or vegetable oil for frying

½ cup chicken broth

¼ cup packed light brown sugar

*Fresh or bottled Key lime juice is acceptable

Combine the lime juice, garlic, and ginger in a jar with a lid and shake well. Place the chicken tenderloins in a gallon ziplock bag and pour the lime juice mixture over the chicken. Seal the bag and marinate in the refrigerator for 30 minutes to 2 hours. Drain the chicken in a colander with a bowl underneath to reserve the marinade.

Preheat the oven to 350°F. Grease a 9 × 13-inch casserole dish with cooking spray.

Place the flour in a large ziplock bag and season it with the garlic powder, ground ginger, salt, and black pepper. Shake until well blended. Add the chicken and shake well until each tenderloin is well coated.

Place about 1 inch of oil in a large skillet over medium heat and warm it to 350°F. Add the tenderloins and fry until lightly browned on each side.

Place the tenderloins in the prepared casserole dish. Pour the broth into the bowl containing the reserved marinade and pour the mixture over the chicken. Sprinkle the brown sugar on top.

Bake for 20 to 30 minutes; the brown sugar will melt and become a crunchy topping for the chicken. Remove from the oven and serve warm or at room temperature.

Marinated Pork Loin with Fig and Champagne Mustard Sauce

I love pork in the fall—to me, it's one of the first things I want when the weather begins to cool a little. This loin can be cooked equally well in the oven, on the grill, or in the smoker. I also like to cook a pork loin for Thanksgiving dinner, just in case anyone doesn't want turkey, and so there will be plenty of leftovers to eat over the busy Thanksgiving weekend.

When my mother and aunts would visit my home in Columbia for the holidays, I'd usually serve dinner at 3:00 p.m., which is the custom in Charleston. Before that, though, I'd cook what my grandmother called a "Big Boy Breakfast" and serve it around 10:00 a.m., so we'd only have two meals that day.

One Thanksgiving, I had beautifully laid out my breakfast room table with my Aunt Mimi's Reynolds Spode china, which featured a gorgeous fruit-and-flower autumnal pattern. Mother's silver flatware and fall linens completed the settings. I'd made a breakfast casserole, and Country Ham Scones rounded out the menu. Mother and Aunt Mimi complimented me on the food and the table setting.

My Aunt Mary always seemed to have an imaginary ticker tape of ideas running above her head. Every now and then, she'd just reach up and grab a topic off of it. It might have been something you had just finished discussing, or something no one had thought about in years. This particular morning, the topic was, "Do you remember that 'possum Momma cooked for Grampa that time for Thanksgiving dinner during the Depression?" She continued with details about how greasy that 'possum tasted. I sat there dumbfounded, trying to figure out exactly what part of my elegantly set table and perfectly prepared breakfast reminded my Aunt Mary of a greasy old 'possum from seventy-five years before! Mother and Mimi also looked sort of dumbstruck. Finally, Aunt Mimi squelched her with a "Sistah' hush!"

In no way should this pork loin remind you of a greasy old possum, but it will remind you that having elderly relatives at holiday tables does tend to keep things interesting.

Makes 8 to 12 servings

PORK LOIN

1 (4- to 6-pound) pork loin

½ cup soy or Worcestershire sauce

½ cup sherry or bourbon

2 tablespoons dry mustard

2 teaspoons dried thyme

2 teaspoons minced garlic

1 teaspoon crushed fresh ginger

FIG AND CHAMPAGNE MUSTARD SAUCE

½ cup Champagne Mustard (p. 78)

½ cup fig preserves

Make the Pork Loin: Drain and rinse any juices from the pork loin and place it in a large ziplock bag. Combine the remaining ingredients in a glass jar, cover, and shake well until fully combined. Pour the contents of the jar into the bag and seal it. Marinate in the refrigerator for 1 to 2 days, turning over several times to ensure the loin is thoroughly marinated.

Preheat the oven to 350°F. Line a roasting pan with foil.

Place the pork loin and the marinade in the prepared pan. Roast for 30 minutes per pound, until the loin's internal temperature reaches 165°F. Remove from the oven and cover with foil to let the temperature continue to rise for a few minutes.

Make the Sauce: Strain the drippings to remove any solids, fat, and grease. Combine ½ cup of the strained drippings, the Champagne Mustard, and the preserves in a small saucepan over medium heat and bring to a boil. Remove from the heat.

Slice the pork loin and pour the Fig and Champagne Mustard Sauce over it. Serve.

Chicken in Champagne Mustard Sauce

Many years ago, some friends of ours had a rather large New Year's Eve party at their home. Their two precious little girls were brought down to tell everyone good night before being put to bed. After the children were back upstairs, one of their guests, who is now a rather prominent South Carolina politician, decided it would be a good idea to push all the furniture against the walls so everyone could dance—the shag, I'm sure, which is the official South Carolina state dance. A champagne toast, balloons, and confetti followed at midnight; a huge time was had by all, with the party ending shortly after 3 a.m.

The next morning, my friend's five-year-old daughter woke him, saying, "I didn't do it." Quite hungover from the night before, he managed to get one eye open and there she was, right at eye level.

"I didn't do it," she said, again and again. When he finally got the other eye open, he asked her what in the world she was talking about.

"The mess . . . downstairs . . . I didn't do it." Bless her heart, she just wanted to get her defense in early that she was NOT responsible for all the chaos.

That precious little girl is now grown, with little girls of her own—I wonder if she's ever awoken to a little voice saying, "I didn't do it."

This Chicken in Champagne Mustard Sauce is elegant enough to serve at a New Year's Eve party. Just make sure you've got a good alibi ready to prove that "you didn't do it" if a really *big* mess breaks out.

Makes 8 servings

8 boneless chicken breasts (see note)

Salt

Freshly ground black pepper

6 tablespoons unsalted butter

2 tablespoons all-purpose flour

1½ cups chicken broth

1 cup half-and-half

1 cup Champagne Mustard (p. 78)

1 teaspoon dried dill

1 teaspoon dried oregano

Cooked wild rice for serving

Season the chicken lightly with the salt and black pepper. Melt the butter in a large skillet with a lid over medium heat. Add a few pieces of the chicken and cook for about 5 to 7 minutes, depending on thickness, turning the chicken until it is light brown in color on each side. Remove the chicken to a plate and repeat until all of the pieces are browned.

Once the skillet is empty, add the flour to the drippings and scrape the bottom of the skillet with a spatula to release any brown bits that are stuck to pan. Stir in the broth until the mixture is smooth and cook for 1 to 2 minutes, until it thickens a little. Add the half-and-half and stir until smooth. Stir in the Champagne Mustard, dill, and oregano and cook until the mixture reaches a slow boil.

Reduce the heat to low and return the chicken to the skillet. Spoon the sauce over the chicken, cover, and cook for 10 minutes. Remove from the heat and serve hot over the wild rice.

NOTE: This sauce also tastes great served over meatballs for a party. Omit the directions for browning the chicken, but follow the remaining directions to make the sauce, adding ½ teaspoon salt and ½ teaspoon freshly ground black pepper. Place 5 pounds of cooked meatballs in a large pot over medium-to-low heat and pour the sauce over meatballs; heat until the meatballs are warmed through. Alternatively, place the meatballs in a slow cooker, pour the sauce over meatballs, and set to warm for several hours before serving.

Christmas Chicken

One year just after Christmas, a friend and I were heading to Beaufort for a couple of days of R and R. A bad wreck had blocked I-95, so we swung over to 17-A to complete our trip. Now, you know you're in a rural part of the South when not even a main highway is an alternative to the interstate—instead, you've got to take the "A," as in an alternative to the alternative highway.

We were happily cruising along about dusk when we spotted Christmas lights ahead. In the yard of a rather ramshackle house sat the remains of a tailgating tent—just the frame, not the canopy—strung with multi-colored Christmas lights. Underneath the brightly illuminated tent frame was a brightly illuminated plastic Holy Family: Mary, Joseph, and baby Jesus. They were surrounded by the rest of the crew, similarly well lit: the shepherds, a *wide* variety of animals, and, in a mash-up of the Christmas story, the Wise Men, who apparently had already arrived despite the fact that the shepherds were still there. I think there was also an angel or two in the mix. I'd never seen a more complete plastic manger scene in all my life.

I wanted to turn the car around to take a picture, but my friend noticed that the homeowner was sitting on the front porch, so she was afraid we'd be shot! We dubbed the whole scene "tailgating baby Jesus," and to this day I regret not taking my life in my own hands to get that picture. The aluminum manger must not have survived the next hurricane or football season, because we've never been able to find it again.

Every time we put up a tailgating tent at a football game, we fondly remember "tailgating baby Jesus" and wonder who brought what to the manger. Did the angels bring the deviled eggs? Did the Wise Men follow a star to find an out-of-the-way fried chicken shack? Did the shepherds bring some barbeque?

This dish makes a colorful presentation to serve for a holiday dinner—especially if you are expecting a multitude of guests at your manger. Serve it with wild rice and steamed or roasted broccoli to make a beautiful plate. If you're planning a holiday party, substitute chicken tenders for the chicken breasts, cut them into large bite-size pieces, cook as directed, and serve in a chafing dish with toothpicks.

The sauce can also be used with a pork loin. Pour the sauce over the pork and bake in a 325°F oven for 30 minutes per pound until the meat reaches an internal temperature of 165°F. You can also slice the loin into boneless chops and follow the same directions for the chicken breasts. The sauce is also good poured over meatballs and heated in a slow cooker.

Makes 6 servings

6 boneless skinless chicken breasts

⅓ cup all-purpose flour

1 teaspoon salt

4 tablespoons (½ stick) unsalted butter

1½ cups whole berry cranberry sauce

¾ cup freshly squeezed orange juice

¾ cup granulated sugar

½ cup finely chopped onions

Finely grated zest of 1 orange

¼ teaspoon ground cinnamon

¼ teaspoon ground ginger

Cooked wild rice for serving

Pound out the chicken breasts to a ½-inch thickness. Combine the flour and salt in a wide, shallow bowl and dredge each chicken breast in the flour mixture. Melt the butter in a large skillet over medium heat. Add a few pieces of the chicken and cook for about 3 to 4 minutes on each side, until it is light golden brown in color.

While the chicken is cooking, combine the remaining ingredients except the wild rice in a small saucepan with a lid over low heat and bring to a slow boil, stirring often to make sure the sugar dissolves. Pour the sauce over the chicken. Cover, reduce the heat to low, and cook for 35 to 40 minutes or until chicken is tender. Serve over the wild rice.

5

Seafood

"Put Up Your Duke's!"

A friend was reviewing an early draft of this cookbook one day when all of a sudden, he clutched his imaginary pearls and asked, in the most discreet tone of voice, "Did you really mean to say Miracle Whip? Didn't you mean Duke's mayonnaise?" I informed him that the Shrimp and Wild Rice Casserole was a recipe from the mother of my best friend, Kitty Windham, and that if Miss Kitty said it was okay to use Miracle Whip, then it's okay to use Miracle Whip.

The confusion was quite understandable, as most Southerners would rather not eat something at all than eat it with a mayonnaise other than Duke's. From the time he was a tiny boy, my brother George loved nothing better than Duke's mayonnaise.

He also loved our beloved Beaufort River, and we spent a lot of time sailing and water skiing on it when we were growing up. After George was diagnosed with non-Hodgkin's lymphoma, he expressed to me his desire to be cremated and have his ashes scattered in the bend of the Beaufort River, near the sandbar. No one in our family had ever been cremated, but I assured him I'd back him up on his wish—but that he'd have to be the one to break it to our mother. Well, as happened often in my family, he somehow never got around to it before he died. Thus, it fell to me to break the news to her.

At first, she was adamant: "Absolutely *not!*" He was going to rest in the family plot in Greer where generations of our family had been buried. I let her ponder the idea for a while, and then I played the *half-and-half* card. The mother of a friend had been cremated, and her request was to have half of her ashes buried in the family plot. (Actually, it was her ex-husband's family plot, but that's a story that could be a whole novel all its own.) The other half of her went off the pier at Folly Beach, down below Charleston. Mother thought about this for a while, and after being reassured by George's longtime partner, Al Boland, that he really did want to be cremated (like I was going to make something like that up), she agreed to proceed with the *half-and-half* plan.

The next day, when we were at the funeral home making the arrangements for George's memorial service, I was seated between Mother and Al. Even though Al was like another son to my mother, she still wasn't too sold on the whole cremation thing. I felt like Henry Kissinger doing shuttle diplomacy back and forth between the two of them. After much negotiation, we were finally ready to enter the room with all the urns and boxes (as opposed to the casket room) to pick out a box for the half of George that was headed to Greer and the family plot.

My brother and his partner owned a florist shop in Columbia for many years, so they had worked with the staff at that funeral home often. Al knew the young man we were meeting with, and right before we got up from the table to enter the urns and boxes room, he asked, "We've never really dealt with cremation before. About how much do you end up with [he meant in terms of the volume of the ashes], so we'll know how much half would be?"

Without missing a beat, the young man replied, "Well, it's about the size of two *Duke's mayonnaise* jars!"

I shot Al a look that said, "George Greene would love nothing better than to spend eternity in a Duke's mayonnaise jar," and Al looked back at me in a way that replied, "If you say that in front of your mother, I will slap you into next week!" For once, I managed to keep control of my mouth, and Mother picked out a tasteful mahogany box.

Still, the box *was* just about the right size for a Duke's jar, and I truly regret to this day that I didn't bring Mother back to my house, sneak back into the Piggly Wiggly (AKA the Social Pig) right next door to the funeral home, and buy George a brand-new glass jar of Duke's mayonnaise for his final resting place. It would have fit perfectly in the box, and Mother wouldn't have had to know a thing about it!

EPILOGUE

While we were at the funeral home, after we chose a lovely mahogany box that I could have predicted blindfolded that Mother would pick out, the aforementioned young man assisting us asked if we wanted a vault for the box and the portion of ashes going to Greer.

"Well, of course we want a vault," was my mother's reply. "We're not going to stick a wooden box directly into the ground." So, sight unseen, we bought a vault.

That Sunday, we went to the family plot in Greer for the burial. I didn't want my mother and aunts to have to stand there after the service while George's ashes were placed in the grave and covered up, so I took them over to my Aunt Peggy's house while Al, my BFF Jane, and another dear friend, David Condon, stayed at the cemetery.

Later, when we returned to the cemetery, Al had beautifully arranged all the floral displays over the gravesite. Jane took me aside and asked, "How much did you pay for the vault?"

"I don't remember. Why do you ask?" I replied.

"Because it was basically just a giant Tupperware container, and they didn't even burp it to get the air out before they sealed it up."

After George died, Mimi, Mary Dob, and Mother all decided that they also wanted to be cremated. When they all passed away within the next two years, I made sure they had real vaults, and not "giant Tupperware containers."

Fast forward several years to one day when my friend Sandy Somerall and I had lunch at Madison's, a restaurant in Port Royal, South Carolina. We were seated where we could see into the kitchen, and what to my wandering eye appeared but a giant plastic container containing—you guessed it—Duke's mayonnaise! My friend who worked there saved it for me, so now, up in my attic, I have my very own personal matching Duke's vault awaiting my demise. The half of *my* ashes headed to Greer will get there in a Duke's mayonnaise jar and matching vault! Aren't I a lucky girl?

Miss Kitty's Shrimp and Wild Rice Casserole

Regardless of your preference for Duke's or Miracle Whip, this yummy dish is great for company or for family food at a funeral, as it will feed a large crowd.

Makes 8 to 10 servings

6 cups water

1½ pounds raw fresh shrimp, peeled and deveined

1 teaspoon salt

1 (5-ounce) box long grain and wild rice

3 tablespoons unsalted butter

1 cup diced celery

2 tablespoons diced onion

1 cup chopped fresh mushrooms

2 teaspoons chopped fresh parsley

1 (10½-ounce) can cream of mushroom soup

⅓ cup whole milk

¼ cup Miracle Whip salad dressing

1 (8-ounce) can water chestnuts, drained and chopped (optional)

4 drops of hot pepper sauce

Preheat the oven to 350°F. Grease a 9 × 13-inch baking dish with cooking spray.

Bring the water to a boil in a pot over medium heat. Add the shrimp and salt, and cook for 3 to 5 minutes, until the shrimp turn pink. Remove from the heat, drain, and set aside.

Cook the rice according to package directions. Remove from the heat and set aside.

Melt the butter in a large skillet. Add the celery and onion and cook for 3 to 4 minutes. Add the mushrooms and parsley and continue to cook until the mushrooms turn brown. Add the soup, milk, Miracle Whip, and hot pepper sauce and stir well. Remove from the heat and stir in the warm shrimp, the cooked rice, and the water chestnuts, if using, until fully combined.

Transfer the mixture to the prepared baking dish and bake for 30 minutes. Remove from the oven and serve hot.

NOTE: This recipe is also a great way to use leftover Frogmore Stew (p. 118). Omit the mushrooms and water chestnuts. Chop 2 to 3 cups of a mix of the leftover shrimp and sausage and 1 cup of corn cut away from the cobs. Mix well and bake according to the recipe directions above.

Corn and Crab Chowder

This was our family's Thanksgiving eve tradition. After my grandmother passed away, we spent most holidays at my house in Columbia. I'd have a big pot of this going on the stove, made with the corn we'd put up the previous summer (p. 74). I could feed my mother and aunts early, and when family and friends dropped by to see them, the chowder would still be warm on the stove and ready for late-arriving guests to enjoy a bowl at their leisure. Aunt Mimi always liked to add a little bit of sherry to hers, just like we do in the Lowcountry with our She-Crab Soup (p. 132).

You can also make the chowder ahead and freeze it—just add everything except the cream and crabmeat. When you're planning to serve it, thaw it in the refrigerator overnight. Reheat it over low heat and add the cream and crabmeat once the mixture is hot.

Makes 8 servings

1 cup (2 sticks) unsalted butter

1 cup all-purpose flour

1 quart chicken or seafood broth

1 teaspoon Zatarain's liquid crab boil

3 to 4 cups fresh or frozen corn

1½ cups cream or whole milk

1 pound lump or claw crabmeat

Sherry (optional)

Melt butter in a large stockpot over medium heat. Add the flour and cook, stirring constantly until the flour is smooth and the mixture begins to thicken, for about 10 minutes. Slowly add the broth, whisking constantly until the flour is dissolved. Add the crab boil and stir. Bring to a gentle boil.

Reduce the heat to low and simmer for 15 minutes. Add the corn and simmer for 15 minutes more. Stir in the cream until well blended. Add the crabmeat, stirring gently so you don't break apart the lumps. Remove from the heat.

Ladle into bowls and add a little sherry to each, if desired. Serve.

Bay Point Oyster Stew

Aunt Mimi didn't like oysters, but she loved oyster stew and Mother's oyster dressing. It was always a race to the table to sit next to Mimi so the oysters she didn't want would make it over to your soup bowl or plate. Once she removed the oysters, she loved the stew!

Mimi's classic Lowcountry oyster stew is very simple to make. Melt a half stick of butter in a saucepan over low heat. If you like onion in your oyster stew (Mimi never did), chop up a large onion and brown it in the butter. Drain a half pint of oysters, reserving the liquid, and add the liquid to the melted butter. Cook over low heat for about 5 to 10 minutes, until it is mostly reduced. Add 3 cups whole milk and 1 cup half-and-half, raise the heat to medium-low, and bring to a simmer (but don't allow it to boil). Reduce the heat back to low, add the oysters, and cook for 5 to 8 minutes, until the edges of the oysters curl. Remove from the heat, season with salt, black pepper, and hot pepper sauce to taste, and serve in shallow bowls with lots of oyster crackers.

This artichoke and oyster stew is a "souped-up" version that's from the old Blue Channel corporation located in Port Royal, South Carolina. It's equally tasty and easy to make—perfect for company or a weeknight meal. Serve with a loaf of good crusty bread.

Makes 4 to 6 servings

4 strips bacon

½ cup chopped onion

¼ cup finely chopped green pepper

½ teaspoon minced garlic

2 (10½-ounce) cans cream of celery soup

1 (14-ounce) can artichokes, drained and chopped

1½ cups whole milk

1 cup heavy cream

1 tablespoon Worcestershire sauce

1 pint oysters, drained, reserving liquid

Fry the bacon in a pan over medium heat until crispy but not overcooked. Remove from the heat and transfer the bacon to a plate lined with paper towels to absorb any excess grease. Set aside.

Add the onion, green pepper, and garlic to the skillet with the bacon grease over medium heat and sauté until softened.

Reduce the heat to low and add the soup, artichokes, milk, heavy cream, Worcestershire sauce and reserved oyster liquid. Stir until well combined and cook for 10 minutes. Add the oysters and simmer for about 5 minutes, until the edges begin to curl. Remove from the heat.

Transfer the stew to serving bowls and crumble the bacon on top of each serving. Serve hot.

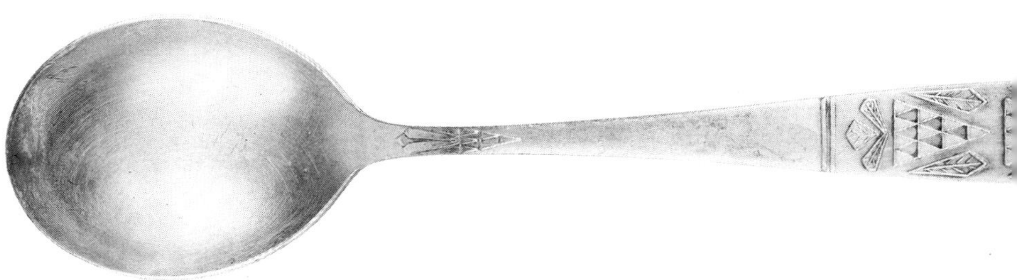

Beaufort Crab Cakes

This recipe is tried and true. It's been changed; I've gone back to the previous version; and I've changed it again over the years. When I was a child, it took me a long time to put together just how crab cakes came to be. We'd go crabbing one day, and several days later, we'd have delicious crab cakes. I guess I just never happened to be in the kitchen to see the crabs go in the pot to be boiled and picked.

One Christmas, I made crab cakes to take to a friend's house in Charleston. We were going to serve them as the first course of a very long, leisurely, and elegant Christmas dinner. We'd already had a few "cheers" when I decided to make the sauce for them, but instead of white wine, I used champagne—very cold champagne in a very hot skillet of melted butter. My host had not been in his new home very long, and the butter and champagne mixture started popping and bouncing everywhere—the cabinets, the stove, the back splash, the ceiling! What a mess! The sauce was good, but neither the crab cakes nor I have been back to Charleston for Christmas. For best results with this recipe, stick with white wine.

When I make this recipe, I always make a double batch using one pound lump crabmeat and one pound claw crabmeat. Fry up as many as you need for your meal; wrap the remainder individually in plastic wrap and freeze them in a large ziplock bag.

Makes 8 crab cakes

1 whole large egg

¼ cup Duke's mayonnaise

2 tablespoons chopped fresh parsley

1 tablespoon Worcestershire sauce or 1 tablespoon Champagne Mustard Salad Dressing (p. 78)

1 tablespoon white wine

2 teaspoons Old Bay seasoning

½ teaspoon dry mustard

(*continued*)

Whisk the egg briskly in a large bowl. Add the mayonnaise and continue to whisk until well combined. Add the parsley, Worcestershire sauce, white wine, Old Bay seasoning, dry mustard, salt, hot pepper sauce, and white pepper and continue whisking until smooth and creamy.

In another large bowl, mix the crabmeat with the panko until well coated (this will keep the panko from lumping together and making the cakes too bready). Add the egg mixture to the bowl containing the crabmeat mixture and stir until just mixed.

Divide the contents of the bowl into 8 portions and shape each into a round patty about ½ inch thick (a #12 scoop works well for this and makes patties that

½ teaspoon salt

Dash of hot pepper sauce

Pinch of white pepper

1 pound crabmeat (lump or claw)

1 cup panko breadcrumbs

4 tablespoons (½ stick) unsalted butter

¼ cup extra virgin olive oil

White Wine Sauce (recipe follows) or Mimi's Tartar Sauce (p. 115) for serving

are of uniform size). Refrigerate for at least 1 hour to set.

Combine the butter and oil in a large, heavy skillet over medium heat and warm until they sizzle. Add the crab cakes to the skillet and fry, turning only once, until golden brown and crispy on each side. Remove from the skillet and transfer to a plate lined with paper towels; reserve the pan drippings to make the white wine sauce (recipe follows). Serve hot with the White Wine Sauce or Mimi's Tartar Sauce.

Alternatively, the crab cakes can be baked in a 400°F oven for 20 to 25 minutes. If baking, the crab cakes don't have to be turned over.

SILVER DOLLAR CRAB CAKES

Makes approximately 50 mini cakes

If you're having a cocktail party, make the crab cakes about the size of a silver dollar using a tablespoon or a #70 scoop. Line a baking sheet with parchment paper or foil and grease it with butter-flavored baking spray. Bake the crab cakes in a 400°F oven for 15 to 20 minutes. The crab cakes can be made ahead, wrapped in plastic wrap, and frozen on the baking sheets until ready to bake.

WHITE WINE SAUCE FOR CRAB CAKES

Makes 1½ cups sauce

1 cup dry white wine

1 teaspoon freshly squeezed lemon juice*

4 tablespoons (½ stick) unsalted butter

1 tablespoon chopped fresh parsley

¼ teaspoon salt

Pinch of white pepper

*Fresh or bottled lemon juice is acceptable

After the crab cakes have been fried, drain all fat from the skillet and add the wine and lemon juice. Return the skillet to medium heat and bring to a boil; boil for about 2 minutes, or until the mixture is reduced by half. Remove from the heat and whisk in the butter, 1 tablespoon at a time. Add the parsley, salt, and white pepper.

Serve the sauce over the crab cakes; this sauce can also be used over grilled fish or chicken.

Shrimp and Onion Sausage with Tasso Gravy and Pimento Cheese Grits

The shrimp and grits commonly served in restaurants across the Lowcountry is often served with a brown sauce. This likely is because of the breakfast shrimp dish that was commonly eaten by working fisherman. They would cook freshly caught shrimp in a sauce made from flour, a little bacon grease, and a little water or leftover coffee, if available. A noted Lowcountry cook once told me folks on Daufuskie and other Sea Islands always made brown gravy for grits because life on a South Carolina barrier island meant that fresh dairy products like butter, milk, or cream weren't always available.

This is my version of brown gravy shrimp and grits. I prefer to use Lee's brand sausage from Orangeburg, South Carolina, a pork and onion sausage that comes in long links that are about an inch thick. It's also great when it's been smoked for a couple of hours. Other kinds of sausage like andouille or kielbasa are equally good in this dish.

The Tasso Gravy can be made ahead and frozen. When you're ready to serve, thaw the gravy. Add a little chicken broth to it, put it in a skillet over medium heat, and bring it to a boil. Reduce the heat to low and stir in the shrimp and sausage, cooking it while the grits are prepared in a separate pot. All the components should be ready about the same time. Serve with a mixed green salad for an easy dinner.

Makes 8 servings

PIMENTO CHEESE GRITS

6 cups chicken broth

2 cups stone ground coarse yellow grits

½ cup whole milk plus more as needed

2 teaspoons salt

1 teaspoon freshly ground black pepper

1 cup good-quality pimento cheese

SAUSAGE

1 pound large-link sausage

TASSO GRAVY

8 tablespoons (1 stick) unsalted butter

½ cup tasso ham, diced

½ cup all-purpose flour

1 quart chicken broth

1 cup freshly brewed coffee

2 tablespoons chopped fresh parsley

2 teaspoons Tony Chachere's Original Creole Seasoning

1 pound raw fresh medium-to-large shrimp, peeled and deveined

Make the Grits: In a medium stockpot over medium heat, bring the chicken broth to a boil. Whisk in the grits until they are well blended into the broth. Reduce the heat to low and cook as directed on the grits package. Add the ½ cup milk and cook for 5 minutes more. Stir in the salt, pepper, and pimento cheese and stir until the cheese is melted; if the grits become too thick, add more milk until desired consistency is reached. Remove from the heat and cover to keep warm.

Make the Sausage: Preheat the oven to 400°F. Line a baking sheet with sides with foil.

Arrange the sausage links on the prepared baking sheet and bake until sausage is firm to the touch, 10 to 15 minutes. Remove from the oven and cut the sausage into ½-inch pieces. (Alternatively, smoke the sausage in a smoker at 225°F for 2 to 3 hours.) Set aside.

Make the Gravy: Melt the butter in a heavy skillet over medium heat. Add the tasso ham and cook for 2 minutes, until it begins to brown. Add the flour and stir well, making a roux, and cook about 3 minutes, until the roux turns brown and begins to smell nutty. Whisk in half the chicken broth until all the flour is dissolved into the broth. Add the remaining broth and the coffee, cook, whisking constantly, until the mixture starts to thicken. Reduce the heat to low and simmer for 20 minutes. Stir in the parsley and Creole seasoning. Add the shrimp and cook for 3 to 5 minutes, just until the shrimp turn pink. Remove from the heat and stir in the sausage.

Place the grits in a serving bowl and top with the shrimp, sausage, and Tasso Gravy mixture. Serve.

Momma's Fried Shrimp

My mother was not born in the Lowcountry, so when she married my father and they later moved to Beaufort, she swore she cried every day for the first six weeks. Now, in her defense, she was also eight months pregnant with my brother George, so raging hormones may have played a part. By the end of her life, you couldn't have gotten her out of Beaufort with a stick of dynamite. She became a true Lowcountry girl and gave birth to one as well: me. She could fry the best shrimp, always accompanied by Sarah Seabrook's Red Rice (p. 72). Don't overcook the shrimp.

Makes 3 to 4 servings

- 1 (12-ounce) bottle beer plus more as desired
- 1½ cups all-purpose flour
- 1 teaspoon salt
- 1 cup seasoned seafood breading mix, such as House Autry brand, or all-purpose flour
- 1 pound medium-to-large fresh shrimp, peeled and deveined
- Canola or vegetable oil for frying
- Sauce for serving (recipes follow)

In a large bowl, combine the beer, 1½ cups flour, and salt and whisk until smooth (the batter should be thick but not paste-like). If you prefer a thinner batter, add more beer. Place the breading mix in a wide, shallow bowl. Dredge each of the shrimp in the breading mix and then dip each in the beer batter. Place on a plate until all of the shrimp have been breaded.

In a skillet (cast iron is preferred), warm 1 inch of the oil to 350°F. Add the shrimp and fry for about 5 minutes, until golden brown. Remove from the heat and serve with Daddy's Cocktail Sauce, Mimi's Tartar Sauce, or Orange Pungent Sauce.

DADDY'S COCKTAIL SAUCE

- ½ cup ketchup or chili sauce
- 2 tablespoons prepared horseradish
- 2 tablespoons freshly squeezed lemon juice
- 1 tablespoon Worcestershire sauce

Combine all of the ingredients in a blender and blend until smooth. Refrigerate until ready to serve.

MIMI'S TARTAR SAUCE

- 2 tablespoons white wine vinegar
- 1 teaspoon dry mustard
- ½ teaspoon salt
- ⅛ teaspoon cayenne pepper
- 1 cup mayonnaise
- ¼ cup chopped dill pickles
- 2 tablespoons finely chopped onions
- 1 teaspoon finely chopped fresh parsley
- 1 teaspoon finely chopped capers (if desired)

Whisk together the vinegar, mustard, salt, and cayenne pepper in a bowl. Whisk in the mayonnaise until well blended. Stir in the remaining ingredients. Cover and refrigerate until ready to serve.

ORANGE PUNGENT SAUCE

- 1 cup orange marmalade
- 2 tablespoons prepared horseradish
- 1 teaspoon freshly grated ginger
- 1 tablespoon freshly squeezed lemon juice

Combine all of the ingredients in a blender and blend until smooth. Refrigerate until ready to serve.

Mussels with Applewood Smoked Bacon over Angel Hair Pasta

This recipe is adapted from a dish served at one of my favorite restaurants in Beaufort. It used to be called their "little skillet" with Prince Edward Island mussels. Whenever I ate there, I always tried to bring home some of the sauce that I could use for a taste test as I tried to replicate it. Eventually, I got it pretty darn close, but there were times when I just wanted to call them up and ask them to bring me a bowl of the sauce and a long loaf of French bread.

Sadly, they now have a new chef, and the PEI mussels are no longer on the menu. We love to make this dish when we go to Maine and get really good fresh mussels. The sauce is also wonderful in a creamy version of Shrimp and Grits (recipe follows).

Makes 4 servings

5 strips thick-cut applewood smoked bacon, diced

½ cup thinly sliced leek

½ cup chopped red onion

1 teaspoon minced garlic

2 cups sliced portobello mushrooms (optional)

2 tablespoons dry vermouth

2 cups half-and-half

1 tablespoon Tony Chachere's Original Creole Seasoning

2 pounds mussels, scrubbed and debearded

Cooked angel hair pasta or 1 loaf French bread for serving

Fry the bacon in a skillet over medium heat until crispy but not overcooked. Remove from the heat and transfer the bacon to a plate lined with paper towels to absorb any excess grease. Set aside.

Return the skillet with the bacon drippings to medium heat and add the leek, onion, and garlic. Cook until tender. Add the mushrooms, if using, and cook until just browned. Add the vermouth and scrape the bottom and sides of the skillet to loosen any vegetables that are stuck to pan.

Reduce the heat to low, add the half-and-half and cook for 20 to 30 minutes, until the mixture thickens. Add the Creole seasoning and bacon and stir well.

Wash the mussels well, being sure to remove any grit. Discard any mussels that have already opened. Once the sauce has reduced, add the mussels to it in a single layer and simmer for 5 to 10 minutes, until the mussels pop open.

Ladle the sauce over the angel hair pasta and arrange the mussels on top, or serve it with a loaf of French bread for sopping up the sauce.

SHRIMP AND PARMASAN GRITS

Make the sauce, substituting white wine for the vermouth. Add the shrimp and cook for 2 to 3 minutes, until they turn pink. Make a double recipe of Parmesan Grits (see recipe for Shrimp and Grits Tarts on p. 36), but do not bake them into tarts. To serve, ladle the grits into bowls and top each serving with the shrimp and sauce.

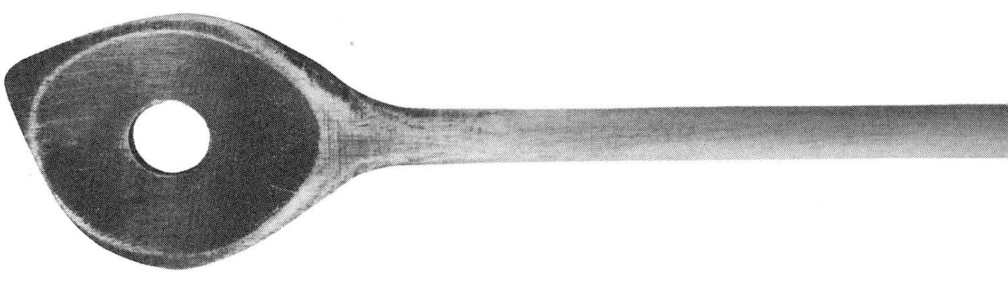

Frogmore Stew

I've never really had a recipe for Frogmore Stew—you just find the biggest pot you own, fill it with water and beer, and bring it to a boil. Add the ingredients and seasonings and voilà: you have Frogmore Stew. However, I've tried to quantify the recipe for folks who've never made it before. But first, a little background.

Whether you call it Frogmore Stew or Beaufort Stew (just *don't* call it a Lowcountry Boil), it originated in Frogmore, South Carolina, the capital of St. Helena Island and the home of Penn Center, the Chapel of Ease, and Fort Fremont. Once upon a time, "Frogmore" was also the name on the local post office, until it was changed in the 1980s to the more accurate and all-encompassing name "St. Helena Island."

The tradition of cooking seafood and fresh produce together dates back many generations amongst the Gullah-Geechee people who have inhabited the Lowcountry of North and South Carolina, Georgia, and northern Florida since their ancestors were enslaved there. The dish was dubbed "Frogmore Stew" in the 1960s by the Gay family of the Gay Seafood Company, located at the far end of St. Helena Island on the Harbor River. When several of the boys in the family were in the National Guard, they'd cook it to feed a lot of hungry Guardsmen in a hurry once they reported for maneuvers at Fort Stewart, down below Savannah. By 1980, it was featured as the Lowcountry supper at the Beaufort Water Festival and appeared on the cover of *Gourmet* magazine. Today, it's widely available at restaurants throughout the region.

A true Frogmore Stew is cooked in at least a fifty-gallon pot over a propane gas tank with a burner attached. I bought a huge pot several years ago with a drainer insert so I could serve large amounts of Frogmore Stew for company in Beaufort. The pot was made by a company from Louisiana, and the first item listed under the instructions was, "Do not operate while consuming alcoholic beverages." Now, that may sound really good to a New York liability lawyer, but how many Bubbas do you know who would be outside cooking over a huge pot in the heat and not be downing a beer or sipping on some bourbon? Clearly, that was written by someone who'd never cooked Frogmore Stew . . . or most anything involving outdoor cooking in the South.

This recipe can be decreased or greatly expanded, which will be dictated by the size of the pot you can find. The usual rule of thumb per person is:

½ pound fresh local shrimp
1 ear corn, shucked and silks removed, broken in half
6 to 12 inches smoked sausage, cut into 2-inch pieces

Some recipes call for adding potatoes to the boil. My family never put potatoes in ours, mainly because we always served it with big bowls of Sarah Seabrook's Red Rice (p. 72) and Momma's Potato Salad (p. 66). Another reason, according to noted Lowcountry cookbook author and food expert John "Hoppin' John" Martin Taylor, is that the starch in the potatoes releases into the water and makes the shrimp harder to peel. If you insist on having potatoes, boil them in a separate pot with some extra seasoning and add them to the stew once it's been dumped out on the table.

Spread out some newspapers and add a roll of paper towels and the table is set. (If you are eating on a "good" table and not a picnic table in the back yard, put a plastic tablecloth underneath the newspaper.) Add Daddy's Cocktail Sauce (p. 114) for the shrimp and softened butter for the corn. A cooler of beer nearby is also a necessity.

And be sure to make extra and use the remainder for Frogmore Stew Dip (p. 29), Wild Rice and Shrimp Casserole (p. 106) or Shrimp and Corn Pie (p. 128).

Makes 8 servings

4 quarts water

1 6-pack beer, the cheaper the better

½ cup Old Bay seasoning, 1 commercial crab boil seasoning bag, such as Zatarain's, or 1 boiling bag Frogmore Stew Spice Mix (recipe follows)

2 lemons, halved

2 pounds hot or mild smoked sausage, cut into 2-inch pieces

8 ears corn, shucked, silks removed, and halved

4 pounds large, fresh, and local shrimp

In a 12-quart stockpot over medium-high heat, combine the water and beer (the pot should be no more than half full) and bring to a boil. Add seasoning and lemons, bring to a full boil. Reduce the heat to medium, add the sausage, and cook for 5 minutes. Add corn and cook for 5 minutes more. Add shrimp and cook for 3 to 5 minutes more, just until shrimp turn pink.

Remove from the heat and drain into a large colander. Spread out on a table covered with newspaper or on a large platter, if you must, and serve.

FROGMORE STEW SPICE MIX

If you'd like to make your own spice bag, it's easy to do with spices and a double layer of cheesecloth.

12 whole cloves
¼ cup coriander seed
¼ cup mustard seed
6 dried bay leaves, crumbled
3 tablespoons dill seed
2 tablespoons whole allspice
1 tablespoon celery seed
1 tablespoon red pepper flakes
2 teaspoons black peppercorns

Combine all of the ingredients in a bowl and mix together. Place the mixture in the center of a double layer of cheesecloth or unbleached muslin. Gather the corners together and tie the bundle securely with kitchen twine.

Shrimp Harpin

Before Lowcountry cuisine became an actual recognized gastronomic category, this was Aunt Mimi's go-to dish for company. Gumbo, crab cakes, red rice, and lots of fried seafood were considered family fare—not something reserved for elegant company dinners.

One of the many copies of this recipe, sort of an upscale version of Lowcountry red rice served with shrimp in a cream sauce, that Mimi had written down was dated 1952. It's still a favorite of mine, although I've enhanced the flavors a little compared to the seasonings Mimi used. It can be assembled earlier in the day and refrigerated until it's time to bake, giving you time to enjoy being with your guests instead of being stuck in the kitchen.

Makes 6 to 8 servings

¾ cup uncooked white rice

2 pounds medium fresh shrimp, peeled and deveined

3 tablespoons vegetable or extra virgin olive oil

1 tablespoon freshly squeezed lemon juice

2 tablespoons unsalted butter

¼ cup chopped green bell pepper

¼ cup chopped onion

¼ cup sherry

1 teaspoon salt

¼ teaspoon freshly ground black pepper

¼ teaspoon freshly grated mace or nutmeg

¼ teaspoon cayenne pepper

1 (10½-ounce) can condensed tomato soup

½ cup heavy cream

½ cup slivered almonds

Sweet paprika

Cook the rice according to the package directions. Set aside.

Preheat the oven to 350°F. Grease a 2-quart casserole dish with butter or cooking spray.

Cook the shrimp in boiling water for 2 to 3 minutes, until they are pink but not fully cooked. Remove from the heat, drain, and transfer to the prepared casserole dish. Sprinkle the oil and lemon juice over the shrimp and toss lightly to coat.

Melt the butter in a large skillet over medium heat. Add the green pepper and onion and cook for about 5 minutes. Add all of the remaining ingredients except the almonds and paprika and stir well. Add the cooked rice and stir again until all of the rice is well coated. Transfer the contents of the skillet to the prepared casserole dish and stir well.

Scatter the almonds and sprinkle the paprika over the top. Bake until the casserole is bubbly and the top begins to brown, about 55 minutes. Remove from the oven and serve hot.

Newberry Oyster Casserole

My father, who was in the Army's vaunted 82nd Airborne Division during World War II, fought in every major battle in which the 82nd was engaged in North Africa and Europe. After the war, he joined an organization called the Forty-and-Eight Club, an offshoot of the American Legion. (The "Forty-and-Eight" name comes from the railroad cars used in France during World War I, which could hold forty men or eight horses.) A lady in Newberry, South Carolina, always made this oyster casserole for Forty-and-Eight Club meetings.

This was around the same time he met and married my mother. She was a dutiful newlywed, helping to prepare the Forty-and-Eight Club dinners. Every Thanksgiving and Christmas, she'd pull out this recipe and recount, "I had to peel a lot of apples and oranges for ambrosia to get that recipe." Apparently, the lady who possessed the recipe did not share it readily. The original recipe calls for a "ten-cent loaf of bread" . . . the going price for a Sunbeam sandwich loaf in 1953.

Makes 12 servings

1 loaf white sandwich bread

1 pint small fresh oysters

2 cups whole milk

1½ cups chicken stock

5 whole large eggs, beaten

1 cup (2 sticks) unsalted butter, melted

1 teaspoon salt

½ teaspoon freshly ground black pepper

Preheat the oven to 350°F. Grease a 9 × 13-inch glass casserole dish with butter or cooking spray.

Working with about 4 pieces of bread at a time, trim the crusts from the bread and cut it into cubes (an electric knife makes this much easier). Place the cubes in the bowl of a stand mixer, or use a hand mixer.

Combine the oysters, including the liquid, and 1 cup of the milk in a small saucepan over medium-to-low heat and cook until the edges of the oysters curl. Watch the mixture carefully and reduce the heat if large bubbles start to form (if the milk comes to a full boil, it will curdle). Remove from the heat and set aside.

Combine the stock and the remaining 1 cup milk in a separate saucepan over medium-to-low heat and cook until the mixture is warm but not boiling. Pour the stock and milk mixture over the bread and beat until smooth. (If you don't have a mixer, this can also be done by hand with a potato masher.) Add the eggs, butter, salt, and black pepper and beat until well blended.

Stir the cooked oysters and milk into the mixture with a spatula. and transfer the mixture to the prepared casserole dish. Bake until set and the top is golden brown, about 1 hour and 20 minutes. Remove from the oven and serve hot.

Seafood St. Helena

The traditional Italian-American Christmas Eve dinner is called the Feast of the Seven Fishes. It is served to break the traditional fasting day of Christmas Eve at midnight with an array of seven or more seafood dishes. The traditional feast may include anchovies, whiting, lobster, sardines, baccala (salted cod), smelt, eel, squid, shrimp, mussels, and clams. Since many of those varieties of seafood aren't readily available (or eaten) in the Lowcountry, my Southern Baptist family didn't quite make seven different seafood dishes. Seafood St. Helena, which contains three of the shellfish that are most readily available in our parts, is our traditional Christmas Eve dinner. I guess that makes it the feast of the three shellfish!

This dish is named for St. Helena Island and St. Helena Sound, which both lie due east of Beaufort. The shrimp and crabs we used typically came straight from the Sound and were often procured by our dear friend Clarence Bradley, who has spent his entire life on St. Helena Island—other than his years of service in the Army during World War II.

Makes 6 to 8 servings

6 cups water

1 pound fresh small-to-medium shrimp, peeled and deveined

1 pound small bay scallops (optional)

1 pound lump crabmeat

6 tablespoons unsalted butter

6 tablespoons all-purpose flour

1½ cups half-and-half

1½ cups whole milk

¼ cup sherry

½ teaspoon salt

¼ teaspoon white pepper or to taste

Dash of freshly grated nutmeg

1 cup freshly grated extra sharp Cheddar

Cooked white rice for serving

Preheat the oven to 350°F. Grease a 9 × 13-inch casserole dish with butter or cooking spray.

In a medium saucepan over medium heat, bring the water to boil. Add the shrimp and scallops (if using) and cook for 3 minutes, until the shrimp are just pink, and the scallops are firm. Remove from the heat, drain into a colander, and set aside. Layer the shrimp, scallops (if using), and crabmeat in the prepared casserole dish.

Return the saucepan to medium heat and melt the butter. Add the flour and stir until it is well incorporated about 2 to 3 minutes (the mixture should be thick). Whisk in the half-and-half and milk until the mixture is smooth and the butter and flour dissolve into the liquid. Cook, stirring often, until the mixture thickens, about 5 to 10 minutes. Add the sherry, salt, white pepper, and nutmeg and stir well. Remove from the heat.

Pour the contents of the saucepan over the seafood and sprinkle the Cheddar. Bake until the casserole is well heated and the Cheddar has melted, 20 to 30 minutes. Remove from the oven and serve over the rice.

Lowcountry Gumbo

This Lowcountry version of gumbo is very different from its New Orleans cousin. *Gumbo* comes from the word for okra in several West African languages—ki ngombo, or gombo for short. Okra and gumbo were part of the African culture brought over by enslaved persons on the Middle Passage. From the Colonial era onward, okra-based stews and gumbos could be found almost everywhere with large populations of enslaved Africans and their descendants.

While trying to sort out the rudiments of Lowcountry gumbo versus Cajun gumbo versus Creole gumbo, I consulted Lester "Daddy" Duhé, my eighth-generation Cajun friend from Reserve, Louisiana. The Duhés lived in Columbia for many years before they moved back to New Orleans. During the time he lived in Columbia, Lester was interviewed by *The State* newspaper about his renowned cooking prowess. When asked about his secret to entertaining, he replied, "Get 'em drunk and feed 'em late."

Lester told me that a Cajun gumbo is made either with a roux or thickened with filé from the leaves of the sassafras tree. His mother didn't like to add filé to the gumbo while it was cooking, because she said it could make it bitter. Okra and a little flour typically serve as the thickener for Lowcountry gumbo. He quoted his mother as saying once, "Nobody south of I-10 would put a tomato in a gumbo." With all due respect to Momma Duhé, nobody in South Carolina east of I-95 would make a gumbo *without* a tomato.

Regardless of the local varieties of gumbo, according to Lester, it was always intended to be a belly filler, a way to stretch what you raised in your garden and caught in the rivers and creeks. Gumbo was farm-to-table long before it ever became a trend. It cooks up in one big pot, so you can always add more ingredients to it if you need to feed more people. If you don't want to use shrimp in this recipe, for example, bone a rotisserie chicken and add the meat to the sauce. When I've really gone all out, I've also added lump crabmeat to the shrimp. Fresh corn cut off the cob and lima beans can also be added to make the pot go further. The sauce freezes well, so you can make it fresh in the summer, when tomatoes, peppers, and okra are plentiful, and enjoy it later, when the weather cools off in the fall and winter.

Oh, and Daddy Duhé's answer to the difference between Cajun and Creole gumbo? "About $10.00 on the entrée menu," according to him.

Makes 8 to 10 servings

1 pound whole medium-to-large shrimp

2 cups chicken stock or seafood broth (see recipe steps)

2 tablespoons unsalted butter

1 large onion, chopped

4 stalks celery, chopped

1 tablespoon minced garlic

1 green bell pepper, chopped

1 red or yellow bell pepper, chopped

2 tablespoons all-purpose flour

1 tablespoon Zatarain's liquid crab boil

1 (16-ounce) can petite diced tomatoes and their juices or two cups of diced fresh tomatoes

1 (8-ounce) can tomato sauce

½ pound andouille sausage, cut into ½-inch pieces (see note)

2 tablespoons dried parsley

2 tablespoons dried thyme

2 tablespoons granulated sugar

3 bay leaves

1 tablespoon Worcestershire sauce

3 dashes of hot pepper sauce

8 to 10 pods okra, chopped, or 1 (15-ounce) bag frozen okra

Salt and freshly ground black pepper to taste

Cooked white rice for serving

Peel and devein the shrimp, reserving the shells for the stock.

Place a large skillet over medium heat and add the shrimp shells. Cook until the shells become pink and then start to turn brown. Add the stock to the pan reduce the heat to low and simmer for 30 minutes. Remove from the heat and strain the stock into a bowl; discard the shells. This will be your shrimp stock. When the shrimp shells aren't available because I am making the gumbo sauce to freeze and will be adding the shrimp later, I substitute seafood stock, which can be found in some grocery stores, or chicken stock.

Melt the butter in a large stockpot over medium heat. Add the onion and cook until translucent. Add the celery and garlic and cook for 2 minutes. Add the peppers and cook for 1 minute more. Add the flour and liquid crab boil to the pot and cook for 2 to 3 more minutes.

Add the reserved shrimp stock, tomatoes, tomato sauce, sausage, parsley, thyme, sugar, bay leaves, Worcestershire, and hot pepper sauce to the pot and bring to a simmer. Cook for 30 to 60 minutes (the longer you cook it, the thicker the sauce will be). Add the okra and cook for 5 minutes more. (At this point, the sauce can be frozen.)

Add the shrimp and cook for 3 to 5 minutes, until the shrimp turn pink. Remove from the heat, season with the salt and black pepper, and serve in serving bowls over the rice.

NOTE: If you want to make your own shrimp stock using the shells, follow the directions for the shrimp essence under the Shrimp with Vegetables and Pasta recipe (p. 130), omitting the reduction after draining the shells. Kielbasa or other sausage can be substituted if andouille is not available.

Shrimp and Corn Pie

Shrimp and Corn Pie is a Lowcountry tradition. The liquid crab boil in this recipe gives it a little heat, but it's not as hot as "gasoline drawers," as Senator Kay Patterson, who served South Carolina as a longtime state senator after many years in the House of Representatives, used to say. Senator Patterson, who was one of the first African Americans to serve in the South Carolina legislature after Reconstruction, was well known for his fiery and colorful orations. The longer his orations went on, the higher pitched his somewhat nasal voice would get.

If he was irrefutably opposed to some piece of legislation, Senator Patterson would pull out one of his favorite sayings: "I will go to hell in a pair of gasoline drawers before I will let this become law." If you ever heard one of Kay's orations on the House or Senate floor, it was a not-to-be-forgotten experience. And long before an advertising campaign with Captain Obvious came along, Senator Patterson could be heard booming, "Wellllll," whenever there was a hilarious or painfully obvious situation to be pointed out.

Deep-dish pie shells come in packs of two, so double the recipe and freeze the second pie. When you're ready to bake, thaw the pie in the refrigerator overnight and then bake according to directions. You'll be glad to always have one ready for company.

This recipe is also a great way to use up leftover Frogmore Stew—cut off the kernels from corn cobs until you have about 1 cup and chop up shrimp and sausage until you have 1 cup. Then, follow the rest of the recipe—except you may want to omit or reduce the amount of liquid crab boil if the stew leftovers are already spicy.

Makes 6 to 8 servings

½ pound cooked shrimp (about 1 cup) roughly chopped (or use a half-shrimp/half-crabmeat mixture)

1 (7-ounce) can shoepeg corn or 1 cup fresh corn

1 tablespoon granulated sugar

½ cup freshly grated Swiss cheese

¼ cup green onion

2 tablespoons all-purpose flour

1 teaspoon liquid crab boil or ½ to 1 teaspoon Old Bay seasoning

½ teaspoon salt

1 uncooked deep-dish pie shell

2 whole large eggs

¾ cup half-and-half

2 tablespoons unsalted butter, melted

Preheat the oven to 350°F.

Combine the shrimp, corn, and sugar in a large bowl and add the Swiss cheese and green onion. Sprinkle the flour, crab boil, and salt over the shrimp mixture and stir well. Transfer the contents of the bowl to the pie shell and smooth out the mixture until it is filled to the edges.

In a separate bowl, whisk the eggs and then add the half-and-half and butter. Pour the contents of the bowl over the shrimp mixture gradually, allowing it to soak in and bake until the top is golden brown and the pie is set, about 1 hour. Remove from the oven and serve hot.

Shrimp with Vegetables and Pasta

Usually the platform for most Lowcountry food is rice or grits, but every now and then we like to change it up and serve pasta with seafood. For this recipe, boiling the shrimp shells down to make a broth, and then further reducing them to make an essence, creates a thick sauce with lots of flavor that is the perfect complement to pasta. The preparation for this dish can be done earlier in the day—making the roux and boiling down the shrimp broth, as well as chopping all the vegetables. If everything is well prepped, the sauce will cook in about the same amount of time as it takes to boil the pasta.

Makes 8 servings

SHRIMP ESSENCE (SEE NOTES)

1 quart water

Shells of 2 pounds shrimp

1 onion

3 stalks celery

½ teaspoon minced garlic

ROUX (SEE NOTES)

2 tablespoons unsalted butter

2 tablespoons all-purpose flour

SHRIMP AND PASTA

8 tablespoons (1 stick) unsalted butter

½ pound fresh mushrooms, chopped

½ medium yellow onion, chopped

½ cup finely sliced green onion

¼ cup minced fresh parsley

(*continued*)

Make the Shrimp Essence: Combine the water, shrimp shells, onion, celery, and garlic in a saucepan over medium heat and bring to a boil. Reduce the heat to low and simmer for at least 1 hour. Remove from the heat and drain into a colander with a bowl underneath. Return the strained liquid to the saucepan and place it over medium-to-low heat. Cook until the liquid reduces to 1 cup. Remove from the heat and freeze the ½ cup not used for this recipe for later use.

Make the Roux: Melt the butter in a small, shallow frying pan over medium-to-low heat. When butter is melted and hot enough for a pinch of the flour to "dance" on the butter, add the remaining flour and cook, stirring constantly with a wooden spoon, for 3 to 5 minutes for a light roux or 5 to 8 minutes for a medium roux. The roux will develop a nutty flavor as it cooks.

Make the Shrimp and Pasta: Melt the butter in a large frying pan over medium heat. Add the mushrooms, yellow onion, green onion, parsley, and garlic and cook for 1 minute. Add the tomato and seasoning. Cook, stirring constantly, for 1 minute more. Add the Shrimp Essence, wine, and roux and cook, stirring often, until the roux dissolves into the liquid. Add the half-and-half, stir, and simmer for about 5 minutes, until the sauce begins to thicken.

- 2 teaspoons minced garlic
- 1 tomato, peeled and chopped
- 3 teaspoons Old Bay or Tony Chachare's seasoning
- ½ cup Shrimp Essence
- ½ cup white wine
- 1 recipe Roux
- 1 cup half-and-half
- 2 pounds fresh medium shrimp, peeled and deveined
- 1 pound bow tie, penne, or orecchiette pasta, cooked according to package directions
- 1 cup freshly grated Parmesan

Add the shrimp to the pan and cook for 3 to 5 minutes, depending on the size of the shrimp (do not overcook). Add the pasta to the pan and toss well. Top with the Parmesan and serve immediately.

NOTES: You can also purchase seafood broth in a grocery store and reduce it to ¼ of its volume to produce the same flavor. If you are using purchased seafood broth, simmer 2 cups of broth until it equals ½ cup.

A roux is roughly equal parts fat and flour. I use butter for fat, but olive oil or bacon grease will also work.

She-Crab Soup

She-Crab Soup is a quintessential Lowcountry dish. It was created in Charleston by William Deas, the butler and cook for the city's mayor on the occasion of a visit by President William Howard Taft in the early 1900s. Apparently, Taft, who was known for his girth and appetite, liked it so much that he took the recipe back to the White House and had it added to the menu.

True she-crab soup contains crab roe, or crab eggs, sprinkled on top. When street vendors roamed the streets of Charleston selling their wares, "SHEEE-crabs" were hawked the loudest because they were the most desirable and therefore the most valuable. In the interest of keeping seafood sustainable, some folks have stopped using crab roe; if it is not available, paprika can lend the soup the same delicate pink hue.

Makes 8 to 12 servings

5 tablespoons unsalted butter

⅓ cup all-purpose flour

1 small onion, finely chopped

1 stalk celery, finely chopped

¼ cup finely shredded carrots

2 teaspoons minced garlic

½ teaspoon salt

¼ teaspoon freshly ground black pepper

8 cups whole milk

2 cups half-and-half

1 cup seafood or chicken broth

½ cup sherry plus more for serving

1 tablespoon Worcestershire sauce

2 teaspoons sweet paprika

1 teaspoon hot pepper sauce

¼ teaspoon freshly grated mace or nutmeg

1 tablespoon cornstarch dissolved in 1 tablespoon water (optional)

1 pound lump crabmeat

¼ cup crab roe, if available

2 tablespoons chopped chives

Melt the butter in a large Dutch oven over medium heat. Stir in the flour until it is fully incorporated and cook for about 3 minutes, until the mixture begins to brown. Add the onion, celery, carrots, and garlic and cook until the vegetables are tender. Season with the salt and black pepper. (If a smooth texture is desired, place the cooked vegetable mixture in a blender or food processor with a little of the milk, pulse until smooth, and then return it to saucepan.)

Whisk in half the milk until the mixture is smooth. Add the remaining milk, the half-and-half, and the seafood broth, reduce the heat to low, and simmer for 30 minutes, stirring frequently so the soup does not stick.

Stir in the ½ cup sherry, the Worcestershire sauce, the paprika, the hot pepper sauce, and the mace. If you desire a thicker soup, add the cornstarch slurry and stir well until thickened.

Add the crabmeat and cook for 10 minutes before serving. Remove from the heat, ladle the soup into bowls, splash each serving with extra sherry to taste, garnish with crab roe, and sprinkle each with the chives. Serve.

Shrimp Burgers

The Gay family has operated a shrimp dock on St. Helena Island, South Carolina, for more than 60 years. These docks were used in the filming of *Forrest Gump* and *The Great Santini.* Across the highway from the seafood docks sits the Shrimp Shack, which is operated these days by descendants of Mrs. Hilda Gay Upton, the original owner; it's been around since 1978.

The specialty of the house is their shrimp burger, and the recipe is a closely guarded secret: they wouldn't even divulge it to their family friend Pat Conroy for his wonderful cookbook. So over the years when I've tried to make my own version of these unique burgers, I'd use a little of this from one recipe and a little of that from another.

Once I got serious about writing this cookbook, I put together a spreadsheet containing all the shrimp burger recipes I've accumulated and compared them side by side. I started experimenting until I created one that I thought was just right—and this recipe is! All the same, if you ever find yourself on Highway 21 on St. Helena Island near the Harbor Island Bridge, you really must personally experience a Shrimp Shack shrimp burger. Tell them the Cheese Biscuit Queen sent you.

Makes 8 burgers

2 tablespoons unsalted butter

3 green onions, thinly sliced

½ cup finely chopped Vidalia or other sweet onion

¼ cup finely chopped celery

1 teaspoon minced garlic

2 pounds shrimp, peeled, deveined, and cooked

1 cup cornbread breadcrumbs (see note)

1 whole large egg

½ cup Duke's mayonnaise

1 tablespoon Old Bay seasoning

(*continued*)

Melt the butter in a large skillet over medium heat. Add the green onions, onion, celery, and garlic and cook for 4 to 5 minutes, until the onion is lightly browned. Add the shrimp and cook for 3 minutes. Remove from the heat and set aside to cool.

Place 1 cup of the cooked shrimp mixture in the bowl of a food processor and process until the mixture is ground up. Add the remaining shrimp mixture and pulse until the shrimp are roughly chopped; do not overprocess at this point. Transfer the mixture to a large bowl, add the cornbread breadcrumbs, and mix well.

In a small bowl, beat the egg. Add the mayonnaise and whisk until fully combined. Add the Old Bay seasoning, parsley, lemon zest, and salt, then whisk until blended. Pour the contents of the small bowl over the shrimp mixture and mix well until the shrimp are thoroughly moistened. Cover and refrigerate for 4 to 8 hours.

- 1 tablespoon dried parsley
- ½ teaspoon freshly grated lemon zest
- ½ teaspoon salt
- 1 cup seasoned seafood breading mix, such as House Autry brand
- Canola or Vegetable oil for frying
- Secret Sauce for serving (recipe follows)
- 8 brioche hamburger buns, 8 slices fresh tomato, and 8 leaves butter lettuce for serving

Shape the mixture into 8 equal-size patties; a #12 scoop will come in handy for this. Place the seafood breading mix in a shallow bowl and coat both sides of each patty in the seafood breading mix. Set each breaded patty on a baking sheet as they are coated.

Place about 1/2 inch of oil in a large frying pan over medium heat and warm it to 350°F. Add the patties, 2 to 4 at a time depending on the size of the pan, and fry until lightly browned on each side, turning only once (be careful not to overcook them). Set each fried patty aside on plates lined with paper towels and keep them in a warm oven until all patties have been fried.

To assemble, spread the Secret Sauce on the bottom of each bun and place a fried patty on top. Top each with lettuce, a tomato slice, and the top of each bun. Serve.

NOTE: To make cornbread breadcrumbs, prepare a batch of packaged cornbread according to package directions. Pour the batter into a 9-inch round cake pan and bake for the time listed on the package. Remove from the oven and set aside to cool. Crumble the cornbread into the bowl of a food processor and process until the pieces are about the size of panko breadcrumbs. This will make more than you need for this recipe; freeze the remainder to use for next time or toast them in oven to use as a topping on casseroles or sprinkled over deviled eggs.

SECRET SAUCE

- ½ cup mayonnaise
- 2 tablespoons ketchup or chili sauce
- 1 tablespoon prepared yellow mustard
- 1 teaspoon sweet pickle relish
- 1 teaspoon dried dill
- ½ teaspoon Worcestershire sauce

Combine all of the ingredients in a blender or food processor and pulse several times until blended. Store in a jar in the refrigerator.

Aunt Lou's Quick Shrimp Curry

In the early 1970s, a very important confluence of events occurred in South Carolina. First, L'eggs pantyhose, which were introduced in 1969, finally made it to Main Street in small towns across South Carolina. About the same time, South Carolina changed its liquor laws from "brown bagging" only to allow liquor by the drink. "Brown bagging" meant that bar and restaurant patrons had to bring their own liquor in brown paper bags and could only buy setups or mixers—they had to mix their own drinks. The change in the law permitted the sale of mini-bottles, the little bottles of alcohol typically served on airplanes. They became widely available at bars, restaurants, and liquor stores across the state.

The third important event, and presumably the saddest, was that Aunt Lou's son became *too old* for the fabulous Easter egg hunts she always held for him and his friends. Now, for most families, *too old* would have entailed turning eleven or twelve, but for Aunt Lou's only child, it meant that he had graduated from the small private college in their hometown in the Piedmont of South Carolina, gotten married, and gone off to Charleston for medical school.

Aunt Lou wasn't really a relative. My father lived with her family in the small town where he first practiced law after World War II. Back then, young bachelors didn't have their own houses or apartments; they roomed in someone's house and took their meals with the family. Aunt Lou was quite the character and was legendary in the small town they lived in. If you asked anyone from that town if they knew her, the usual reply was "Oh, good God, yes!" But she was a very important part of our childhood, and she and her family were lifelong friends of my family.

Aunt Lou loved to garden; in fact, her yard was featured in a book of historic South Carolina gardens. At first, she moped around about not having the annual Easter egg hunt, feeling very, very sad, but then genius struck! Since her husband ran the McCrory's drugstore on Main Street, she had him save all the L'eggs pantyhose containers that arrived damaged. Next, she went—or, more likely, dispatched her hubby—to the liquor store to buy a variety of mini-bottles, which she placed inside the L'eggs containers. Then she hid them in her award-winning garden. When her nearest and dearest friends showed up for bridge club that week, they got to hunt in the garden for the eggs and, as the story goes, slammed quite a few of the L'eggs contents that very afternoon. It was an afternoon that still lives in infamy in that small town.

I'd told my friends this story for years, and we've enjoyed several Aunt Lou Easter egg hunts in my back yard in Columbia. One time, I had to get creative when our friends' children were getting a little too old for Easter egg hunts—not quite off to college, but they were teens and preteens who thought they were too cool for such activities. I hid money in traditional plastic Easter eggs and told the kids they could hunt for anything waist-high or lower. For older kids, the prospect of finding the golden egg with $5.00 in it was motivation enough for them to hunt. After they finished, it was time for the adults to hunt for anything waist-high or higher: the mini-bottles hidden in the yard that sadly couldn't be concealed in panty-hose eggs. (Darn it, they changed the packaging over the years!)

The kids sat up on the deck and helped guide their parents below to find the mini-bottle prizes. Those kids are all of legal drinking age now, and they still talk about the mini-bottle hunt in my back yard. They've asked if I will do another one, so they can reap the benefits now that they're old enough to enjoy the spoils of their hunting!

This was Aunt Lou's recipe for shrimp curry. When we'd go visit, we'd always take along several pounds of shrimp for her freezer, which was the old ice cream freezer from the McCrory's store, with six little doors on top instead of one great big one. Serve with your favorite condiments, such as chopped cashews or peanuts, raisins, chopped hard-boiled eggs, chopped tart apples, chutney, and coconut.

Makes 4 servings

- 1 tablespoon unsalted butter
- ½ cup chopped onion
- 1 (10½-ounce) can condensed cream of shrimp soup
- 1 cup sour cream
- ½ teaspoon mild yellow curry powder
- 1 pound fresh medium shrimp, peeled and deveined
- 3 cups cooked white rice
- Sweet paprika
- Choice of condiments for serving

Melt the butter in a saucepan over medium heat and add the onion. Cook until tender but not browned. Add the soup and cook, stirring often, for about 2 to 3 minutes, until smooth. Stir in the sour cream and curry powder. Add the shrimp and cook for 3 to 5 minutes, until the shrimp turn pink. Remove from the heat.

Scoop equal amounts of the rice into serving bowls and evenly distribute the shrimp curry over the rice. Sprinkle the paprika over each serving. Serve with your choice of condiments.

6

Cookies, Bars, and Candies

"Mr. Assistant Senate Security"

Baking is something that truly helps me relax. For me, it represents creativity, meditation, and worship all in one. If I'm focusing on baking, I'm not focusing on anything else that is causing me stress. And at the end of it, I usually have something I am going to share with someone else, so it's also about friendship and fellowship.

During one particularly stressful legislative session, I started baking cookies every Wednesday and taking them to the State House for my lobbyist colleagues. When I left lobbying, everyone in the lobby was most concerned—not necessarily because they were going to miss me, but they were surely going to miss those cookies. I assured them that I would still bring them, maybe not every week, but often. After a few years, I finally got them weaned back to a couple of times a year—usually around the budget weeks, when days can get long and tempers short. Everyone has their particular favorites, but chocolate chip pecan is the universal choice of everyone at the State House!

Now, technically, there is what is known as the "J. Verne Smith Rule," which forbids eating in the second-floor lobby area of the State House. However, my cookies have been grandfathered in with Senate security, which turns a blind eye to those eating them during late-night sessions and budget weeks when sessions go long. I think they would rather ignore the rule than have a bunch of ravenous, hungry, and ill-tempered folks in the lobby.

One year, one of the younger members of the Senate security staff was feeling his oats and took it upon himself to remind me of the J. Verne Smith Rule, telling me the cookies really weren't allowed. I took Mr. Assistant Senate Security (ASS) at his word and ceased bringing cookies to the lobby. Several weeks later, when the budget was on the Senate floor for debate, there was nary a cookie in sight. Monday passed with no cookies, and the same thing Tuesday. By Wednesday, I decided that since I wasn't going to be taking cookies up to the State House, I'd go ahead and head to Beaufort for the Easter weekend.

In lovely Walterboro, South Carolina, about halfway to Beaufort, I stopped to take a picture of something and noticed that a lobbyist friend to whom I had recounted the conversation with the Senate security person had posted on Facebook about the reason why there were no cookies. That set off a firestorm in the lobby and within the Senate chamber. Another friend, a Senate staffer who was on the inside of the chamber, went to the chairman of the Judiciary Committee, who happened to be a HUGE fan of my chocolate chip pecan cookies. Expressing his immediate displeasure at the news, the chairman instructed the staff to advise the sergeant at arms that his directive was not to stand. At about the same time, all parties involved figured out the identity of the person who told me I could no longer bring cookies and converged on Mr. ASS outside the Senate chamber.

A few minutes later, I got a call from Mr. ASS. He profusely apologized and begged me to bring cookies to the lobby—post haste! He made it sound like a scene was unfolding akin to the *Frankenstein* movie in which the townspeople hunted the monster with torches and pitchforks. His distress indicated that he was somewhat in fear for his life.

With some degree of false sincerity, I explained to him how terribly sorry I was to say that I'd already left town for the rest of the week, and that the only way there would be cookies at the State House that night was if they sent the SLED (that would be the South Carolina Law Enforcement Division) helicopter down to Beaufort to pick them up—which I, of course, knew would not happen!

Happily, Mr. ASS escaped with his life, and cookies are allowed in the State House lobby once again. And for the brief, shining moment that lasts as long as the cookies last, all is right with the world, or at least in the lobby.

Best-Ever Chocolate Chip Pecan Cookies

Makes 5 dozen

1 cup butter-flavored vegetable shortening or 1 cup plain vegetable shortening and ½ teaspoon butter extract

¾ cup granulated sugar

¾ cup packed light brown sugar

2 whole large eggs

2 teaspoons vanilla extract

2¼ cups all-purpose flour

1 teaspoon baking soda

1 teaspoon salt

1 cup chopped pecans

3 cups chocolate chips

Preheat the oven to 350°F. Grease 2 or more baking sheets with butter or baking spray with flour.

Using a hand mixer or stand mixer on medium-high speed, cream together the shortening and sugars. Add the eggs and vanilla, beating well until they are fully incorporated into the sugar mixture.

In a separate bowl, sift together the flour, baking soda, and salt. Gradually, by heaping spoonfuls, add the flour mixture to the sugar mixture, mixing well after each addition. Add the pecans followed by the chocolate chips, mixing until they are well distributed in the dough.

Using a tablespoon or a #70 scoop, drop the dough onto the prepared baking sheets. Bake until the cookies are lightly browned, 10 to 12 minutes, but do not overbake—if you do, the cookies will be hard. Remove from the oven and set aside to cool for 5 minutes on the baking sheets. Transfer to wire racks to cool completely. Serve or store in an airtight container for up to a week.

Note: The dough can also be scooped into balls and frozen on cookies sheets. I use foil pans from the Dollar Tree to freeze a dozen or so balls on a sheet. They can then be pulled out and baked whenever you need a nice warm treat. The already-baked cookies can be frozen also.

Chocolate-Covered Bourbon Truffles

Lala was one of the loveliest South-of-Broad Charleston matrons I ever knew. She was originally from Alabama, and she returned there often to visit her sister-in-law, Totsy, whose husband (Lala's brother) had passed away. Totsy lived in the area of Alabama known as Tornado Alley, and one day, Lala and Totsy had just poured their afternoon bourbons when the tornado sirens went off. They grabbed their cocktails and took refuge in the designated tornado shelter for the house, the powder room under the stairs. The ladies hunkered down while the storm raged, with one resting on the toilet and the other perched on the vanity. The storm went on and on, and after a while, they had finished their drinks.

"I sure would like another cocktail to calm my nerves," said Lala.

"But if a tornado hits, the bottle might break and hurt us," said Totsy.

"Hell, Totsy, the mirror would shatter and kill us first. Now go get the damn bottle of bourbon!" Lala replied.

If you ever find yourself in a similar situation, these bourbon truffles contain no glass but sure will help calm your nerves during a tornado, hurricane, or whatever other peril may befall you. For a twist, why not try them with one of the new flavored bourbons, such as pecan or salted caramel?

Makes 30 balls

TRUFFLES

- 2 cups cookie crumbs of your choice (vanilla wafers, shortbread, or chocolate graham crackers)
- 1 cup chopped pecans
- 1 cup confectioners' sugar
- ⅓ cup bourbon, rum, or brandy
- 3 tablespoons unsweetened cocoa powder
- 2 tablespoons light corn syrup

Make the Truffles: Line a baking sheet with parchment paper.

Combine all of the ingredients in a large bowl and mix until well blended. Using a tablespoon or a #70 scoop, shape into 1-inch balls. Place the balls on the prepared baking sheet and refrigerate for at least 1 hour.

Make the Coating: Combine the chocolate chips and cream in a microwave-safe bowl and heat on high for 1 minute. Stir well. Continue to heat on high in 30-second intervals until all of the chips are melted, making a smooth coating.

Line a baking sheet with wax paper. Remove the chilled truffles from the refrigerator and roll each in your hands until smooth. Using a toothpick, wooden skewer, or candy dipping tool, dip each truffle in the coating

COATING

1 cup semi-sweet chocolate chips

1 tablespoon heavy cream

mixture, hold the truffle over the chocolate mixture to allow the excess chocolate to drain away. Place each on the prepared baking sheet. Refrigerate for at least 2 hours until set. Keep refrigerated. Store in a airtight container and let "ripen" for a least a week before serving.

Triple Peanut Butter Cookies

My dad, Felix Bailey Greene, was the first family court judge for Beaufort County during the late 1960s and 1970s. At that time, family court judges also held some civil and criminal court cases in their counties. One particular lawyer was the bane of my father's existence: he hailed from the upper Midwest and was one of the first big-time trial lawyers in Beaufort County. The lawyer, who we'll call "Mr. Shark," was a very flashy dresser who wore shiny sharkskin suits with dark shirts and loud ties to court. At the time, my father still believed that the only court-appropriate attire was a dark suit, a white shirt, and a skinny little gray or maroon tie.

Mr. Shark had a client who had been most *dreadfully* injured by something in a Coca-Cola bottle that chipped her front tooth. According to a friend who was a young lawyer at the time, the Coca-Cola Bottling Company offered to settle the case for "far more than it was worth" before going to trial, but Mr. Shark thought he had a winner. He put his client on the stand and went on at great length about how *grievously* injured she had been by the bottle of Coca-Cola, and the *only* way something could have caused this injury was for it to have been placed there by the Coca-Cola Bottling Company.

The Coca-Cola Bottling Company was represented by Mr. T. Reeves Sams the Umpteenth, the scion of one of Beaufort's oldest families. I am sure Mr. Sams was dressed in a dark suit accompanied by a white shirt and an appropriate tie: think the late South Carolina Senator Fritz Hollings meets Atticus Finch in *To Kill a Mockingbird.*

During cross examination, Mr. Sams asked Mr. Shark's client if she had "entered any foreign objects into her bottle of Coca-Cola." She replied that she didn't know what a "foreign object" was.

Mr. Sams asked her, point blank, "Did you put anything into your bottle of Coca-Cola?"

Miss Client replied, "Why yes, I put a pack of Lance peanuts into the bottle," like it was the most normal thing in the world, because don't all good Southerners put peanuts in their bottles of Coca-Cola?

Well, not being from the South, Mr. Shark never thought to ask his client if *she'd* put anything into her bottle of Coca-Cola. My friend who related this story said that Mr. Shark all but leapt across the plaintiff's table to ask my father for a recess so he could confer with his client. Daddy granted the recess and told the jury that he was going to have the bailiff bring him a pack of crackers—and a Coca-Cola—and asked them if they would like anything, too.

Mr. Shark was not one to ever give up on a fight, so after the recess, he subjected his own client to a strenuous cross-examination of the particulars of this practice, which only served to further reveal his ignorance of the ins and outs of this cultural phenomenon and dig the hole he was already in deeper and deeper. Shortly thereafter, the case went to the jury, which found for Mr. Sams and the Coca-Cola Bottling Company. The case was dismissed. Although Daddy and Mr. Shark are both gone now, this story lives on in the legal circles of Beaufort County—at least among the group who were all young lawyers there in the 1970s.

These cookies are so tasty that when they're consumed with a Coca-Cola, you have no need to enter any "foreign objects" into your bottle.

Makes 5 dozen cookies

1 cup butter-flavored vegetable shortening or 1 cup plain vegetable shortening and 1 teaspoon butter extract

¾ cup packed light brown sugar

¾ cup granulated sugar

¾ cup peanut butter

2 whole large eggs

3 tablespoons whole milk or buttermilk

1 teaspoon vanilla extract

2½ cups all-purpose flour

1 teaspoon baking soda

½ teaspoon salt

1 (12-ounce) bag peanut butter chips

1 cup chopped peanuts

Preheat the oven to 350°F. Grease 2 or more baking sheets with butter or baking spray with flour.

Using a hand mixer or stand mixer on medium-high speed, cream together the shortening and sugars. Add peanut butter and cream until smooth. Then add the eggs, milk, and vanilla, beating well until they are fully incorporated into the sugar mixture.

In a separate bowl, sift together the flour, baking soda, and salt. Gradually add the flour mixture by the heaping spoonful to the sugar mixture, mixing well after each addition. Mix in the peanut butter chips and peanuts until they are fully combined.

Using a tablespoon or #70 scoop, drop the batter onto the baking sheet. Bake until the cookies are lightly browned, 12 to 15 minutes; do not overbake, or the cookies will be hard. Remove from the oven and set aside to cool for 5 minutes on the baking sheets. Transfer to wire racks to cool completely. Serve or store in an airtight container for up to a week.

Creamy Pralines

When I was growing up, my maternal grandmother's sendoff each time I'd leave her house was either to remind me to be *"cute and sweet and pretty,"* or she'd say, "You be sweet and play pretty." Mine may have been the last generation of Southern children who were often lucky enough to grow up living next door to their grandparents and thus bear the benefits of their tutelage.

Now, the admonishment to be "cute and sweet and pretty" should not be confused with "catching more flies with honey than you can with vinegar," which suggested that you wanted the fly to perform some purpose or activity on your behalf once it was caught. "Cute and sweet and pretty" was the attitude with which my grandmother expected me to approach that day, and each day afterward, until it became a philosophy of life.

Over the years, along with several of my contemporaries who also grew up in the shadows of their Southern grandmothers, I have come to realize that "cute and sweet and pretty" is the Southern grandmother's version of karma, the theory that people generally get what they deserve in life—good or bad. Being "cute and sweet and pretty" naturally attracts good karma to you, and of course, your grandmother *never* thought you would do anything that would attract bad karma.

This has devolved into the Cute and Sweet and Pretty (CSP) lecture, which we have delivered to children, godchildren, and other friends over the years whenever they are wanting to seek revenge on someone for some particular act or slight. The CSP lecture assures them that person *will,* in fact, ultimately do themselves in, without any help from someone who's embraced the CSP philosophy. Gran-Gran knew well that Dorothy Parker's old adage, "Hatred's filling, but it isn't nourishing," was quite true. Applying the CSP philosophy of being present and in that front-row seat when they do themselves in is *much* more satisfying, and the enjoyment received from it lasts *much* longer than what any revenge could possibly deliver.

The CSP lecture goes something like this: "Now honey, when someone's ugly to you, you have to continue to be cute and sweet and pretty to them, because when they do themselves in, and *you know they will,* if you're not cute and sweet and pretty to them, you won't have the front-row seat [*"front-row seat"* might be punctuated by a gentle and almost inaudible hand clap with each word] to see it, and you *know* you want to have that *front. row. seat!"* A *really* good CSP moment includes "a front-row seat and a box of popcorn." One of our friends contributed the *ne plus ultra* of CSP moments, which is "a front-row seat with a box of popcorn and an extra-large Diet Coke," followed by three snaps of the fingers in a Z shape across one's body.

When the moment of karma is delivered, we refer to that as a "Cute and Sweet and Pretty moment," as in "Boy, did I get a Cute and Sweet and Pretty moment today when so and so got what was coming to him." If a day has been particularly trying, we will say, "I have just about used up all the Cute and Sweet and Pretty I have to give today."

I knew I was successful in spreading the gospel of CSP when I once convinced a retired military man that in fact, it *was* much more satisfying to be seated in the front row when his adversaries do themselves in, as opposed to being the one who delivers the blows and catches hell for it.

These pralines are about as Cute and Sweet and Pretty as you can get. In New Orleans, they say "PRA-leans" ("'Pra-' rhymes with 'bra,'" as Lester "Daddy" Duhé, an eighth-generation Louisianan, explained it to me), but in the Lowcountry, we typically say "PRAY-leans," as in what you do in church. Either way, they are delicious, and they'd be a wonderful substitute for popcorn in any CSP moment!

Makes 8 to 10 pralines

1½ cups granulated sugar

½ cup packed light brown sugar

½ cup whole milk or buttermilk

3 tablespoons light corn syrup

3 tablespoons unsalted butter plus more for preparing wax paper

48 small marshmallows

1 teaspoon vanilla extract

2 cups pecan halves

Place a sheet of wax paper or parchment paper on the countertop. Grease with softened butter.

In a large saucepan over medium heat, combine the sugars, milk, and corn syrup and bring to a boil. Boil until a little of the mixture dropped in cold water forms into a soft ball (once the mixture reaches 240°F to 245°F, measured with a candy thermometer). Remove from the heat.

Add the butter, marshmallows, and vanilla and beat with a wooden spoon until the mixture is smooth, the marshmallows are melted, and the mixture loses its gloss. Add the pecans and stir until they are well coated. Using two tablespoons, quickly drop portions of the mixture, using one spoon to scoop from the pan and the other spoon to slide the mixture from the first spoon onto the paper at least 2 inches apart, allowing each some room to spread. Set aside to cool completely.

Store in an airtight container for up to 1 week (in theory, anyway—they *never* last that long without being eaten!).

Everybody's Favorite Caramel Popcorn

There once was a lawyer-legislator from the "Pee-Dee" region of South Carolina whose clients were never guilty. They only *allegedly* committed some criminal act . . . so this is my "*allegedly*" story.

In the dark ages of 1984, before most college football games were on cable television, whenever the Gamecocks played our archrival, the Clemson Tigers, in an away game, we'd have to go to the old Carolina Coliseum to see the game on closed-circuit TV. On this particular Saturday, the Gamecocks were down by three touchdowns (with one missed extra point): 20 to nothing. We may or may not have commenced drinking early that morning, perhaps even sneaking a flask into the game. I may have *allegedly* been a little overserved by the end of the first quarter. I may or may not have gotten sick in a friend's popcorn box and I may or may not have had a nice long nap in the Carolina Coliseum. While I may or may not have been napping, the Gamecocks scored one of the greatest fourth-quarter comebacks in the Carolina–Clemson history and I awoke to see us win the game 21 to 20.

Well, among our crowd, no one was talking about the game afterward, as they were too busy talking about me and the *alleged* popcorn box incident. My birthday was about two weeks after that, and one of my friends gave me a huge hot-air popcorn popper—not because I loved popcorn so much, but because of the box it came in! Christmas was about two weeks after that, and I may or may not have made everyone caramel popcorn as a joke. *Well*, the joke ended up being on me, because everyone *loved* it—particularly my Aunt Mary, who I'm pretty sure never heard the story behind it.

For the past thirty-five years, I have *allegedly* made this popcorn every year at Christmas. You can take the story with a grain or two of popcorn salt—and I'll stick to the best two words that came out of the Iran-Contra affair during the Reagan administration—"plausible deniability."

This also makes a very popular Halloween treat or Christmas gift. My friend Lynn Stokes Murray requested a "feed bag" of it one year for Christmas, which I obliged with a ziplock bag and a ribbon strap to hold it around her neck!

Makes 5 quarts (20 [1-cup] servings) or 1 giant feed bag

20 cups freshly popped popcorn, unsalted (about ¾ cup un-popped corn)

2 cups unsalted nuts (peanuts, pecans, cashews, and/or almonds)

2 cups packed light brown sugar

1 cup (2 sticks) unsalted butter

½ cup light corn syrup

½ teaspoon baking soda

½ teaspoon vanilla extract

½ teaspoon salt

Preheat the oven to 250°F.

Mix together popcorn and nuts in a large non-stick or greased roasting pan.

Bring the brown sugar, butter, and corn syrup to a boil in a large saucepan over medium heat and boil for 5 minutes, taking care to prevent it from scorching. Remove from the heat and add the baking soda (the baking soda makes the caramel appear fluffy), vanilla, and salt. Stir well.

Pour the mixture over the popcorn and nuts and stir until well coated. Bake, stirring every 15 minutes to be sure the mixture is well coated and that it doesn't stick together, for 1 hour. Remove from the oven.

Place several pieces of wax paper on counter and turn out the popcorn and nuts onto the paper. Separate the pieces with a large spoon and allow to cool completely. Store in an airtight container or airtight ziplock bags for up to a week.

Irish Cream Brownies

My mother and Aunt Mimi used to make a variation of these brownies using crème de menthe, which made the filling layer green. One year for St. Patrick's Day, I decided to replace the crème de menthe and its green coloring with Irish cream liqueur for a different flavor that still maintained the Irish theme. These brownies are very versatile: you can substitute amaretto, Grand Marnier, or crème de menthe for the Irish cream to make variations. They can also be made ahead and frozen, either leaving them in the pan and wrapping it well with plastic wrap or cutting them into squares and storing them in an airtight container.

Makes 6½ dozen

BROWNIES

1 cup semi-sweet chocolate chips

8 tablespoons (1 stick) unsalted butter

⅔ cup all-purpose flour

¼ teaspoon baking soda

¼ teaspoon salt

2 whole large eggs

⅔ cup granulated sugar

2 tablespoons Irish cream liqueur

1 teaspoon vanilla extract

¾ cup ground pecans or almonds

FILLING

¾ cup (1½ sticks) unsalted butter, softened

2 tablespoons Irish cream liqueur

2 cups confectioners' sugar

(continued)

Make the Brownies: Preheat the oven to 325°F. Line an 11 × 17-inch baking sheet with parchment paper or foil and grease the parchment paper or foil with butter or baking spray.

Combine the chocolate chips and butter in a microwave-safe bowl and heat on high for 1 minute. Stir well and heat on high for 1 minute more, until the chips are completely melted.

In a separate bowl, sift together the flour, baking soda, and salt and set aside.

Using a hand mixer or stand mixer on medium speed, beat the eggs and then gradually add in the sugar. Beat in the Irish cream liqueur and vanilla. Add the melted chocolate mixture and beat until well combined. Add the flour and pecans and beat until well combined.

Spread the batter into the prepared pan and bake for 20 to 25 minutes. Remove from the oven and set aside to cool in the pan.

Make the Filling: Using a hand mixer or stand mixer on medium-high speed, whip the butter and Irish cream liqueur together until smooth. Add the confectioners' sugar and beat on high speed for 2 minutes, until light and fluffy. Spread the filling over the tops of the cooled brownies. Refrigerate until set.

GLAZE

1 cup semisweet chocolate chips

8 tablespoons (1 stick) unsalted butter

1 tablespoon Irish cream liqueur

Make the Glaze: Combine the chocolate chips and butter in a microwave-safe bowl and heat on high for 1½ to 2 minutes, depending on the wattage of the microwave. Stir until the mixture is smooth and the chips are melted. Add the Irish cream liqueur and stir until it is completely blended into the chocolate. Spread the mixture over the top of the brownie filling (the mixture is thin enough to be brushed on with a pastry brush if desired to smooth it).

Cut the brownies into 1-inch squares (a wheel-style pizza cutter makes cutting the brownies easier and keeps the layers from separating). Refrigerate until ready to serve, and store any leftovers in the refrigerator.

Key Lime Cake Bites

These cake bites, also known as cake pops, were all the rage several years ago. The omission of the stick and the addition of alcohol for extra flavor makes this a more grown-up version. These are always a hit as a little something sweet for a cocktail party. It's like a bite of your favorite cake and a cordial all rolled into one sweet morsel.

One of my goddaughters loves these so much, I threatened to someday make her a wedding cake out of them. It would be like a giant croquembouche, a French wedding cake traditionally made of cream puffs, except that instead of cream puffs, it would have cake balls stacked up like a giant Jenga game. Many variations of the recipe are listed below.

Makes approximately 80 cake bites

1 (18.25-ounce) box lemon cake mix

4 whole large eggs

½ cup Key lime juice

1 (3-ounce) package lime-flavored powdered gelatin

⅓ cup vegetable oil

¼ cup light rum

1 (16-ounce) tub cream cheese frosting

3 cups white chocolate chips

3 tablespoons plain vegetable shortening or coconut oil

Preheat the oven to the temperature on the cake mix box. Grease a 9 × 13-inch baking pan with butter or baking spray with flour.

Using a hand mixer or stand mixer on low speed, beat together the cake mix, eggs, Key lime juice, gelatin, oil, and rum until well blended. Increase the speed to medium and beat for 2 minutes more. Pour the batter into the prepared pan and bake according to package directions. Remove from the oven and set aside to cool.

Line a baking sheet with sides with wax paper. Crumble the cake into the bowl of a stand mixer and add the frosting. Mix on medium-high speed until the cake and frosting are well combined and smooth. Using a tablespoon or a #70 scoop, drop the mixture onto the baking sheet. Refrigerate for at least 1 hour.

Combine 1 cup of the white chocolate chips and 1 tablespoon of the shortening in a microwave-safe bowl and heat on high for 1½ to 2 minutes, depending on the wattage of your microwave. Stir well. If the mixture is not completely smooth, continue to heat on high in 30-second intervals until all of the chips are melted, making a smooth coating.

Remove the balls from the refrigerator and roll them in your hands to smooth them. Dip the balls into the melted chocolate one at a time until they are completely coated (a dipping tool, which can be found at most craft stores or online, will make the process easier; a toothpick or skewer inserted into the ball will also make it easier to dip). Hold the dipped ball over the bowl for a moment to allow the excess chocolate to drain. Return each fully coated ball to the prepared baking sheet to set.

Repeat the process of melting the white chocolate chips and shortening and coating the balls as needed. The cake balls will sometimes shed crumbs and the chocolate will become messy, so it is helpful to refresh the chocolate as you work; if you melt it all at once, the chocolate may also cool off before all of the balls are dipped. Refrigerate the fully coated balls until all of the chocolate is set.

Note: If you want an added touch that will make them look even more professional, combine 1 cup semi-sweet chocolate chips and 1 teaspoon shortening in a microwave-safe bowl and heat on high for 1½ to 2 minutes, depending on the wattage of your microwave, until melted. Dip the tines of a large dinner fork into the melted chocolate and drizzle it over the balls in a back and forth motion.

To make other combinations, follow the package directions for the cake mix, but substitute ½ cup of the desired liqueur (see the chart below) for part of the amount of water called for in the cake mix's directions (that is, if the mix calls for ¾ cup water, use ½ cup liqueur and ¼ cup water).

CAKE MIX	ICING	LIQUEUR	COATING
Chocolate	Chocolate	Amaretto or Irish cream	Semi-sweet chocolate
Red velvet	Cream cheese	Godiva chocolate	Semi-sweet chocolate
Carrot cake	Cream cheese	Frangelico	White chocolate
Lemon	Lemon	Limoncello	White chocolate
White	Coconut	Coconut rum	White chocolate; sprinkle with fresh coconut while the white chocolate is still wet

Chocolate Drops

One of my mother and Aunt Mimi's *big* pet peeves was people who wouldn't share their recipes. Among many Southern women, that is just a major sign of being ill-mannered and impolite. They used to say, "A recipe that is not shared dies with you, but when it's shared, it lives on after you for many years to come." Someone in Columbia, who shall remain nameless, was famous for these chocolate drops. I knew what was basically in them, but she'd never share the recipe. Imagine my surprise when I found them in a Christmas cookbook one year! Just goes to show, there are very few things you can keep secret in the South.

Makes about 100 depending on size

- 2 cups semi-sweet chocolate chips
- 1 (14-ounce) can sweetened condensed milk
- 2 tablespoons unsalted butter
- 1 cup all-purpose flour, sifted
- 1 cup chopped pecans
- 1 teaspoon vanilla extract

Preheat the oven to 350°F.

Combine the chocolate chips, condensed milk, and butter in a microwave-safe bowl and heat on high for 1½ to 2 minutes, depending on the wattage of your microwave. Stir well until the chips are completely melted. Add the flour, pecans, and vanilla and stir well.

Using a teaspoon or #100 scoop, drop the mixture in small rounds about the size of a quarter onto an ungreased baking sheet (alternatively, you can place the mixture in a pastry bag with a small coupler but no tip and squeeze into small Hershey Kiss like shapes onto the baking sheet).

Bake for 6 to 7 minutes; do not overbake, as the drops should stay soft. Remove from the oven and set aside to cool for 5 minutes on the baking sheets. Serve or store in an airtight container for up to a week, or the drops may be frozen for up to a month.

Scotcharoos

When I was just about finished with this cookbook, I let a friend read it. My friend commented, "You didn't share the Driving Miss Hillary story," so here goes. Early on in 1992, shortly before Gennifer Flowers and the *60 Minutes* "I'm not some little housewife standing by my man" interview, several friends of mine were already supporting Bill Clinton for president. I was leaning toward Bob Kerrey, the senator from Nebraska who was best known as a former Navy SEAL and had won the Congressional Medal of Honor—and for dating the actress Debra Winger.

One cold January day, my Clinton-supporting friends roped me into driving Hillary Clinton around for the day. "You'll just love her," they said. "Y'all care about and work on the same issues—education and health care. You'll really enjoy spending time with her and getting to know her." I'd worked around political campaigns all my life and was used to political spouses like Tunky Riley, Peatsy Hollings, and Tipper Gore, so I agreed.

Hillary, Bill, and Chelsea attended Phil Lader's New Year's Renaissance festival on Hilton Head Island, South Carolina. They flew by private jet to Columbia, where we were to meet them at Eagle Aviation, the private airfield at Columbia Metropolitan Airport. As I mentioned previously, it was cold by Columbia standards, so I pulled my car around and turned on the heat. Hillary, Chelsea, and some male reporter that was following Hillary around that day all piled into the back seat of my car. The first words out of her mouth were, "It's crowded and it's hot back here." Now, it's not like I was driving a Mini Cooper or something. I had a Buick LeSabre at the time. I wanted to say, "Well, if one of y'all would pile your happy self in the *empty* front seat up here, it might not be," but I resisted. So, hot and crowded, off we went.

Our first stop was to drop Chelsea off at the home of Columbia's mayor, Bob Coble. She was going to spend the day with Columbia's first lady, Beth Coble, and the six Coble children, who were lovingly referred to as the Coble-ettes. The eldest two Coble-ettes were impeccably behaved girls, and Chelsea was right between their ages. The youngest Coble-ettes were four typically wild little boys. We pushed Chelsea in the door, spent about five minutes getting her acquainted with the Coble-ettes, and we were off again. Up to that point, Chelsea had only known living in the Arkansas governor's mansion with round-the-clock security protection. I had this vision of her hanging off the dining room chandelier, trying to escape whatever mischief the boys were up to.

We made several rounds of meetings—one at the Party headquarters, to file the paperwork for the South Carolina Presidential primary; a luncheon at Columbia College; and a few other stops. All the while, Miss Hillary and the reporter were piled in the back seat, talking, and she had yet to say *pea turkey* to me, other than barking out directions. Later in the day, we went to the Claussen's Inn so she could rest a bit, and she reconnected with Governor Clinton. The reporter came down while I was sitting in the lobby waiting on Miss Hillary and started asking me questions about the campaign, what I did, etc. He asked if my driving her indicated that the association I worked for was supporting Clinton for president, to which I replied, "No, it didn't even mean that I was personally supporting Clinton."

There was a late-afternoon heavy-hitter fundraiser at the historic Seibels house in Columbia, so I ended up driving both Bill and Hillary to the reception (again, both piled into the back seat; we'd somehow lost the reporter by this point). Bill got in the car and immediately began asking questions: "Who are you? What do you do?"

I replied that I was the director of government relations for the South Carolina Education Association, the National Education Association affiliate in South Carolina. He asked lots of questions about SCEA and NEA's recently revised endorsement process: How did I think the newly implemented changes will work in individual states? Who did he need to talk to in South Carolina? Etc., etc., etc.

Hillary sat there, looking like, "I didn't know she was in charge of that." I wanted to say to her, "I would have told you if you'd ever asked," but I didn't.

They attended the heavy-hitter fundraiser and a dinner afterward at the USC faculty house. Governor Clinton headed to the airport, Hillary and I retrieved Chelsea, and I returned them to the Claussen's Inn.

I'd been toting them around for about fourteen hours at that point. As they were getting out of my car (again, the back seat), Hillary looked at me and said, "I haven't eaten anything all day. We passed a grocery store down there; would you go get me some milk and cereal?"

No "please," no nothing. By this point, I'd had enough of Driving Miss Hillary. Fortunately, I had one filter left and didn't say what was going through my head, which was not just "no," but "Oh, *hell* no!"

I told her with my best, fakest sincerity that I was *so sorry,* but that I was already overdue to go meet some friends in the bar across the street and just wouldn't be able to manage that.

And . . . everyone knows the end of that story. Bill Clinton went on to win the presidency. Hillary went on to become First Lady, United States Senator, Secretary of State, and the first female nominee for president of any major political party. The Cobles still have a lovely thank-you note from Chelsea hanging in their front hall, and those wild Coble boys have all grown up to be fine young men. The campaign flunky that actually did go get her some cereal ended up working in the White House for several years during Clinton's first term.

And that reporter who was piled into the hot back seat of my car? A few years after Bill Clinton took office, a fictional tell-all book came out called *Primary Colors,* written by "Anonymous." A few months later, "Anonymous" was revealed to be none other than Joe Klein—the reporter who sat in my crowded back seat that cold January morning.

These tasty bars take basic cereal treats to a whole new level. Maybe they could have sweetened me up that day, and I'm sure Hillary would have chowed down on some if I'd happened to have had a tin of them in my trunk! The peanut butter, chocolate, and butterscotch flavors blend so well that they'll remind you of a favorite candy bar. A large pizza cutter makes it easy to cut these bars.

Makes 5 dozen

1 cup light corn syrup

½ cup granulated sugar

1 ⅓ cups smooth peanut butter

4 cups Rice Crispies cereal

1 (6-ounce) package semi-sweet chocolate chips

1 (6-ounce) package butterscotch or peanut butter chips

Grease a 9 × 13-inch pan with butter and set aside (for easier cutting, line the pan with parchment paper or foil and grease the paper).

Combine the corn syrup and sugar in a large saucepan over medium heat and bring to a full boil. Remove from the heat, add the peanut butter, and stir until it is fully melted. Add the cereal and mix well. Pour the mixture into the prepared pan and press down evenly.

Combine the chocolate and butterscotch chips in a microwave-safe bowl and heat on high for 1½ to 2 minutes, depending on the wattage of your microwave, until melted. Stir until fully combined. Spread the mixture over the top of the cereal. Set aside to cool completely. Cut into 1 × 2-inch portions and serve.

Oatmeal Raisin Walnut Cookies

We all know that food can be comforting. It can also be healing—healing in the physical sense, as well as healing in the relationship sense. During the last year I was lobbying for SCEA, I had a knock-down, drag-out, no-holds-barred battle with the chairman of the Employee Benefits Subcommittee in Ways and Means. He'd proposed something that the association I worked for vehemently opposed, and we both let it become personal. One day at lunch, we ended up sitting back to back in adjoining booths at a hole-in-the-wall restaurant and yelling at each other over the back of the banquettes. Mutual friends who loved us both tried to convince us that if we'd sit down and talk, we could probably work it out, but we were both dug in (and maybe just a teensy, tad stubborn), so neither of us would hear of it. It turned out to be his last year in the legislature as well as my last year of lobbying full time.

Fast forward a few years. I was working with several colleges, universities, and associations doing their grassroots operations to get their alumni and members involved in the legislative process, and he was working in a lobbying firm with two of my very dear friends. I had weaned my constituency of cookie lovers in the lobby back from getting my cookies every Wednesday to just a couple of times during session—usually during budget weeks, when days are long and particularly stressful. Oatmeal raisin cookies were the cookie *de jour,* and my former adversary 'fessed up that they were his favorites—and that my oatmeal cookies were his favorite of all. After that, we got to be good friends. If I'd just known he could be swayed with oatmeal raisin cookies, a lot of unpleasantness could have been saved for us both.

Makes 5 dozen

- 1 cup butter-flavored vegetable shortening or 1 cup plain vegetable shortening and ½ teaspoon butter extract
- 1 cup granulated sugar
- 1 cup packed light brown sugar
- 2 whole large eggs
- 2 tablespoons whole milk or buttermilk
- 1 teaspoon vanilla extract
- 1½ cups all-purpose flour
- 1 teaspoon baking soda
- 1 teaspoon ground cinnamon
- 1 teaspoon salt
- 3 cups quick-cooking oats
- 1 cup chopped walnuts
- 1 cup raisins

Preheat the oven to 350°F. Grease 2 or more baking sheets with butter or baking spray with flour.

Using a hand mixer or stand mixer on medium speed, cream together the shortening and sugars. Add the eggs, milk, and vanilla, beating well until they are fully incorporated into the sugar mixture.

In a separate bowl, sift together the flour, baking soda, cinnamon, and salt. Add the flour mixture to the sugar mixture and mix until combined. Add the oats and mix well. Add the walnuts and raisins and mix well.

Using a #70 scoop or tablespoon, drop portions of the dough 2 inches apart onto the prepared baking sheet(s). Press down each portion lightly. Bake until lightly browned, 10 to 12 minutes. Remove from the oven and set aside to cool for 1 minute on the baking sheets. Transfer to wire racks to cool completely. Serve or store in an airtight container for up to a week.

Piggy Candy Bites

A group of friends and I were debating one night over what the perfect food was, and we could only narrow it down to two options. The sweets faction argued that chocolate is the perfect food. The savory crowd argued for bacon. In order to make everyone happy, I came up with these tasty bites. They are easy to make and are always a big hit at parties. A friend of mine once said that he was "eating them like it was my job!"

Makes 112 (1-inch) pieces

56 Keebler Club butter-flavored crackers

1 cup (2 sticks) unsalted butter

1 cup packed light brown sugar

1 cup bacon bits

½ cup chocolate chips

1 teaspoon plain vegetable shortening

Preheat the oven to 400°F. Line a 12 × 18-inch baking sheet with sides with foil. Grease the foil with baking spray with flour.

Place the crackers in the prepared pan in rows, with 7 crackers in the shorter side of the pan and 8 crackers in the longer side.

Combine the butter and brown sugar in a saucepan over medium heat and cook for 5 minutes, stirring often until the sugar dissolves and mixes completely with the butter. Carefully pour the sugar mixture over the crackers and spread with an offset spatula to ensure all the crackers are covered. Sprinkle the bacon bits evenly over the sugar mixture. Press down lightly on the bacon using the off-set spatula to make sure it is in the sugar mixture. Bake for 8 to 10 minutes.

While the bars are baking, combine the chocolate chips and shortening in a microwave-safe bowl and heat on high for 1 minute. Stir well. Continue to heat on high in 30-second intervals until all of the chips are melted, making a smooth coating.

Once the bars are baked, remove them from the oven and set aside to cool in the pan for 1 to 2 minutes. Carefully remove the bars from the pan by lifting out the foil. Place the bars, still on the foil, on the counter. Dip the tines of a large dinner fork into the melted chocolate and drizzle it over the bars in a back-and-forth motion.

While the bars are still hot and before the toppings set, cut them into 1-inch pieces with a sharp knife or a rolling pizza cutter. Serve. While they are best made the day of serving, they can be stored in an airtight container in the refrigerator for 1 or 2 days.

Toffee Cookies

These are the favorite cookies of Mark Keel, chief of the South Carolina Law Enforcement Division (SLED). SLED is South Carolina's equivalent of the FBI. I've known Mark since he was a member of lieutenant governor Mike Daniel's security detail as a young man just beginning his career at SLED. The day Mark was named chief, I sent him an entire batch of these cookies to congratulate him.

A friend and I got to talking some time after that, and she said I could probably get a "get-out-of-jail-free" card from Mark because he loves these cookies so much. Upon further thought, we decided he is *way* too honest for that, but if I ever did commit a crime, he'd make sure I got a really nice job in prison—working in the prison kitchen baking cookies!

Makes 7 dozen

1 cup (2 sticks) margarine
1 cup granulated sugar
1 cup packed light brown sugar
1 cup vegetable oil
1 whole large egg
1 cup quick-cooking oats
1 cup Rice Krispies cereal
1 cup coconut flakes
1 teaspoon vanilla extract
3½ cups all-purpose flour
1 teaspoon baking soda
1 teaspoon cream of tartar
¾ teaspoon salt
1 (8-ounce) package Bits O'Brickle English Toffee Bits, with or without milk chocolate

Preheat the oven to 350°F. Grease 2 or more baking sheets with butter or baking spray with flour.

Using a hand mixer or stand mixer on medium-high speed, cream together the margarine and sugars. Reduce the speed to medium-to-low and add the oil in a steady stream. Once the oil is fully incorporated, increase the speed to high and beat for 1 minute until entire mixture is fluffy. Add the egg and mix until well blended. Add the oats, Rice Krispies, coconut, and vanilla and stir until well combined.

In a separate bowl, sift together the flour, baking soda, cream of tartar, and salt. Gradually add the flour mixture in heaping spoonfuls to the sugar mixture, mixing well after each addition. Add toffee bits and mix until well blended.

Using a tablespoon or a #70 scoop, drop the dough onto the prepared baking sheets. Bake until the cookies are a light, sandy color and not browned, 10 to 12 minutes, but do not overbake—if you do, the cookies will be hard. Remove from the oven and set aside to cool for 5 minutes on the baking sheets. Transfer to wire racks to cool completely. Serve or store in an airtight container for up to a week. Cookies may also be frozen for up to a month.

Lemon Sherry Tea Cakes

My hometown had a wonderful character named Dottie McDaniel, who would knock on your door and say, "Are you receiving?" as in, "Are you accepting company?' I can't imagine anyone ever told Dottie that they were not receiving. She was a combination of a Southern lady and an impish sprite—truly a free spirit. Her lifelong motto was, "I was born to be a person of good cheer." Dottie drove around Beaufort in her yellow Volkswagen bug convertible, and when the local police strongly suggested that she no longer drive, she swore that she cut up her license into "a hundred pieces," because according to her, "I knew I'd want to drive again!" She traded the convertible for a three-wheeler bicycle on which she tootled all over town.

When they were young newlyweds, our friends Rick and Sandy Somerall rented the downstairs apartment of Dottie's beautiful and historic home. Sandy was a young schoolteacher and Rick a young Marine lieutenant when they were interviewed by Dottie and her friends over sherry one afternoon to see if they would be acceptable tenants. They swore that Dottie had a secret entrance to the apartment, as she would just pop in at various times and places when they had not expected her to be there. They also claimed that Dottie stockpiled empty sherry bottles in a closet in their basement with an eye toward turning them into drinking glasses, long before anyone was into recycling.

Dottie appointed herself as the guardian of the local carriage tour horses years before Beaufort or Charleston instituted guidelines for their care. Dottie's home was on the prescribed tour route, and Dottie would sit on her front porch and yell at the drivers if she thought it was too hot for the horses or if she felt they were otherwise being mistreated. The drivers really had no choice but to go by Dottie's house, as the City of Beaufort required them to follow that specific route.

Dottie also once had city public works employees tote broken pieces of sidewalk they'd just torn up around to her back yard and had them stack up the pieces into a water feature—once she added the garden hose. To celebrate her new water feature, Dottie hosted a Jester Party, which featured people dressed as jesters sitting in the trees and reciting poetry. Dottie, who was well into her seventies at the time, climbed up into a tree herself for a recitation.

When Dottie sold her home and moved into a townhouse, she lamented the loss of her beautiful back yard. She'd also sold her car by that time, so she turned the two paved parking spaces that went with the unit into what she called her sky room, a beautiful outdoor space with benches, a fountain, potted plants, an arbor, and even a tree planted through a hole someone bored through the concrete. Dottie entertained often in her sky room, and when she went on to an assisted living facility, pieces of the sky room accompanied her to beautify the space outside her room. Delighted that she was still able to enjoy their beauty, she told one of the staff members, "Wasn't I lucky to have had two sky rooms in one lifetime?" That was Dottie—always seeing the positive in everything.

After Dottie had grown older and her memory had begun to fade, Sandy went to visit her one day near Valentine's Day. Sandy gave her a card that said, "Wild at Heart." Dottie looked at Sandy and asked, "Was I wild?" Oh, yes, Dottie, just like Max in *Where the Wild Things Are,* you were the wildest one!

To celebrate the spirit of Dottie, make a batch of these lemon sherry cakes, call up a group of friends, and tell them you are "receiving." Tree climbing and poetry recitation are optional.

Makes approximately 84 tea cakes

TEA CAKES

1 (18¼-ounce) box lemon cake mix

1 (3.4-ounce) box lemon pudding

1 cup sour cream

4 whole large eggs

⅔ cup sherry

⅔ cup butter-flavored vegetable shortening

GLAZE

6 tablespoons (¾ stick) unsalted butter

3 tablespoons lemon juice

1 tablespoon sherry

2 cups confectioners' sugar

Make the Tea Cakes: Preheat the oven to 350°F. Grease 7 miniature muffin tins, each with 12 (1¾-inch) wells, with baking spray with flour.

Using a hand mixer or stand mixer on high speed, beat together all of the ingredients for 4 minutes. Drop 1 tablespoon of the batter into each well of muffin tin. (Use a #50 scoop to make filling the wells easier and to get them to a uniform size.) Bake for 8 to 10 minutes. Do not overbake; the cakes should stay a lemon-yellow color and should not turn brown. Remove from the oven and set aside to cool for about 5 minutes. Turn out the tea cakes onto a sheet of wax paper. (Tapping the tins against the countertop will make dislodging them easier.) Set aside to cool completely.

Make the Glaze: Place the butter in a large microwave-safe bowl and heat on high for 1 to 1½ minutes, depending on the wattage of your microwave, until melted. Add the lemon juice and sherry and stir well. Add the confectioner's sugar and stir until there are no remaining lumps.

Dunk the top of each tea cake in the glaze and place each glazed tea cake on a sheet of wax paper to set. Serve or store in the refrigerator on a baking sheet. The tea cakes can also be frozen. Store in an airtight container with wax paper placed between layers to avoid sticking.

7

Cakes, Pies, and Other Treats

The Garden Club Goes Astray

My mother belonged to one of the local Garden Clubs, along with a wonderful group of other ladies. I can remember Mother being atwitter at times about having to deliver a program or make a flower arrangement for the meetings.

Apparently, at one meeting, the garden club went astray. At a meeting in the early 1970s, they invited the local drug cop from the Beaufort Police Department to give a presentation to the Garden Club on the *evils of marijuana.* He lit a joint for them to smell, so if their little darlings came home smelling like weed, they'd be able to recognize the aroma and know what their children had been up to. One of the members of the club, a lady who we'll refer to as Marigold, somehow convinced the policeman to let her take what was left of the joint home with her because her housekeeper also had teenage daughters, and she wanted her to be able to recognize the smell, too.

Once she returned home with the joint, Marigold and Janiebelle, her housekeeper, decided that they needed to have the full experience so they could be sure if their little darlings were up to something.

"How did he say they do it?" asked Janiebelle conspiratorially.

"He said they get in the car and roll up all the windows," replied Marigold.

So off they went to Marigold's back yard, a half a block off one of Beaufort's busiest streets. They got in the car with all the windows rolled up, lit what was left of the joint, and put it in the car's ashtray.

Now, the reason I know this story is because Janiebelle related it to Marigold's son at his mother's visitation . . . almost as if she had a deep, dark secret that she needed to get off her conscience. When she'd finished telling Sonny about it, he asked, "Well, did y'all feel anything from it?"

"No," replied Janiebelle. "We sat in the car and we laughed, and we laughed, and then we were hungry, so we went inside and cooked up all the food in the house!"

That had to have been one of the best Garden Club meetings ever! I'm not sure what Mother served that night, but the pie that follows was one of her favorites for entertaining.

Soul-Satisfying Chocolate Meringue Pie

Makes 6 to 8 servings

PIE

- 4 tablespoons (½ stick) unsalted butter
- 1 (4-ounce) bar unsweetened chocolate, chopped
- 4 large egg yolks (reserve the whites for the meringue)
- ½ cup whole or evaporated milk
- 1 teaspoon vanilla extract
- 1½ cups granulated sugar
- 1 tablespoon all-purpose flour
- 1 9-inch deep-dish pie shell, unbaked

MERINGUE

- 4 large egg whites at room temperature
- ½ teaspoon cream of tartar
- 8 tablespoons (½ cup) granulated sugar
- ½ teaspoon vanilla extract

Make the Pie: Preheat the oven to 450°F.

Place the butter and chocolate in a microwave-safe bowl and heat on high for 1½ to 2 minutes, depending on the wattage of your microwave, until completely melted. (Alternatively, melt the butter and chocolate together in the top of a double boiler until the mixture is completely melted and smooth.) Stir until the chocolate and butter are completely blended.

Using a hand mixer or stand mixer on medium speed, beat together the egg yolks, milk, and vanilla. In a separate bowl, sift together the sugar and flour. Gradually add the flour mixture to the egg yolk mixture and beat until smooth. Add the chocolate mixture and beat until well blended.

Pour the resulting mixture into the pie shell and bake for 10 minutes. Reduce the oven temperature to 350°F and bake for 30 to 40 minutes until the center is set. Remove the pie from the oven but leave the oven on.

Make the Meringue: While the pie is baking, allow the egg whites to come to room temperature. Using a hand mixer or stand mixer on high speed, beat the egg whites until they are foamy. Add the cream of tartar and beat until soft peaks form. Gradually add the sugar, 1 tablespoon at a time, until it fully dissolves into the egg whites and glossy peaks form that do not fold back over on themselves. Add the vanilla and mix just until incorporated into the meringue.

Spread the meringue over the top of the pie, making sure to spread it to the edges of the crust, creating a seal that prevents the meringue from shrinking while baked. Return to the oven and bake until the meringue is light brown, 12 to 15 minutes. Remove from the oven and set aside to cool for 30 minutes. Serve.

Carrot Cake Three Ways

"If thou of fortune be bereft,
and in thy store, there be but left
two loaves, sell one, and with the dole
buy hyacinths to feed thy soul."

—John Greenleaf Whittier

My best friend, Jane, had the most marvelous mother-in-law ever. Anna Laurie Frazer Key—Mother Key—loved Jane from the moment she met her. (What's not to love, right?) Randomly, after Jane and Robert married, Jane would receive a letter in the mail from Mother Key with a check enclosed, and in the "for" section, it simply said "hyacinth money." The letter would usually contain these stipulations: Jane was to spend the money solely on herself and to spend it on something frivolous that she would not normally indulge in or buy. Her intent was for Jane to make it a real treat!

I've always thought that was such a beautiful tradition. Mother Key worked on Capitol Hill in Washington, DC, during World War II, and her brother would send her checks, which she dubbed her "hyacinth money" after the Whittier quote I mentioned above. She carried on the tradition with Jane, and Jane keeps her memory alive by planting dozens of hyacinth bulbs every fall. The flowers come up early every spring to remind us of her wonderful mother-in-law. Every now and then, you must treat yourself and indulge in a little hyacinth money.

This cake is a wonderful spring treat, just as the hyacinths are blooming.

Makes 12 to 16 servings or 72 mini cakes

CAKE

1 (15¼-ounce) package yellow cake mix

3 whole large eggs

½ cup water

⅓ cup vegetable oil

⅓ cup packed light brown sugar

2 teaspoons ground cinnamon

2½ cups shredded carrots

½ cup raisins

½ cup chopped pecans or walnuts

GLAZE

2 ounces cream cheese, softened

2 tablespoons whole milk

1 teaspoon vanilla extract

1 cup confectioners' sugar

Make the Cake: Preheat the oven to 350°F. Grease a tube pan with butter or baking spray with flour.

Using a hand mixer or stand mixer on low-to-medium speed, beat together the cake mix, eggs, water, oil, brown sugar, and cinnamon for 30 seconds, until the batter is moistened. Increase the speed to high and beat for 2 minutes. Add the shredded carrots, raisins, and nuts; reduce the speed to medium; and beat for 1 minute, until well blended.

Pour the batter into the prepared pan and bake until the top is golden brown and the cake springs back when pressed, about 1 hour. Remove from the oven and set aside to cool for 20 minutes; invert the pan onto a cake plate. Cool the cake completely.

Make the Glaze: Using a hand mixer or stand mixer on high speed, beat together the cream cheese, milk and vanilla for 1 minute. Add the confectioner's sugar and beat for 2 minutes until it is combined and there are no lumps, adding more milk if the glaze is too thick.

Pour the glaze over the cooled cake and set aside for 30 minutes, until fully set. Serve or store in refrigerator for 2 to 3 days

LAYERED CARROT CAKE

CAKE

Carrot Cake (recipe above)

CREAM CHEESE ICING.

6 ounces cream cheese, softened

⅓ cup unsalted butter, softened

1½ teaspoons vanilla extract

3½ cups confectioners' sugar

3 tablespoons milk plus more as needed

Make the Cake: Preheat the oven to 350°F. Grease 3 (9-inch) round cake pans with butter or baking spray with flour. Prepare the cake batter as described above. Equally divide the cake batter among the prepared pans and bake 30 to 40 minutes until the cakes bounce back when pressed. Remove from the oven and set aside to cool.

Make the Icing: Using a hand mixer or stand mixer on high speed, cream together the cream cheese and butter until completely smooth. Add the vanilla, beating until it is well incorporated into the mixture. Reduce the speed to medium; add the confectioners' sugar, ½ cup at a time; and beat until well combined. Add the milk and beat until well combined; if the icing is too thick, add more milk until it is the desired consistency. Raise the speed to high speed and beat for 5 minutes, until the icing is light and fluffy.

Frost the cooled cake between each layer and on the sides and top. Serve or store in refrigerator for 2 to 3 days.

MINI CARROT CAKES

These are perfect for a dessert buffet. You will need a batch of carrot cake batter and a batch of cream cheese icing from the recipes above.

Prepare the cake batter as described above.

Grease 7 miniature muffin tins, each with 12 (1¾-inch) wells, with baking spray with flour. Using a #70 scoop or a tablespoon, drop portions of the cake batter into the prepared wells. Bake until the cakes spring back when pressed, 15 to 20 minutes. Remove from the tins while the cakes are still warm and set aside to cool on wire racks.

Once the cakes are completely cool, apply the cream cheese icing to each using a pastry bag fitted with a large star tip. Serve or store in the refrigerator for 2 to 3 days.

NOTE: All these cakes may be made ahead and frozen for up to a month.

Dessie's Blueberry Cobbler

My family was very blessed to have Odessa "Dessie" Cabbagestalk Williams Jenkins in our lives. Dessie moved to Beaufort the day my older brother George was born in 1956 and started working with our family two weeks later. She stayed with us for the next thirty-seven years.

Dessie was part of my life from the day I was born, and I was with her on the day she died at the age of ninety. My mother returned to teaching when George started school and I was two years old, so Dessie was pretty much my world when I was a child. I loved Dessie with all my heart, even though I thought she was going to make me wear white ankle socks to school until I was grown. When I would grab a Coca-Cola on the way out the door to high school every morning, Dessie would admonish me, saying, "You can't drink no Coke for breakfast!"

When I was lobbying—often when I'd had a particularly rough day—I'd get a phone call with her number on the caller ID. I always answered, needing to hear the voice on the other end. She'd say, "How's my baby doing? I've been studying about you all day." That was her way of saying that I'd been on her heart.

After Dessie retired, she moved back to her hometown of Sumter, and I visited her often to help her with things around the house. One day when I was going to check on her and bring her some Christmas presents, I tried to get my goddaughter to ride along with me; I think Windy was about six at the time. I secretly wanted Windy to keep Dessie entertained while I got everything done. Windy dug her heels in and wouldn't go, almost to the point of hurting my feelings. I hadn't gotten all the way to Sumter yet when her mother called to tell me why Windy said she wouldn't come with me.

"I thought Miss Dessie would want Aunt Mae-Mae all to herself," was her reason, and you know what? The child was right. She knew something that I couldn't see. Ever since then, Windy and I have used "want you all to herself" as a euphemism for when we need some one-on-one time with each other.

Dessie made the absolute best blueberry cobbler in the world. Of course, Dessie never measured anything—she just *knew* how much of everything to put in it. One day, my mother watched her make one and tried to approximate the amounts she was using. This is Dessie's recipe, as written by my mother. Blueberry cobbler was always my brother George's favorite—find out why under the Peach Cobbler recipe (p. 178).

Makes 8 to 10 servings

- 1 (14.1-ounce) box refrigerated pie crust (contains 2 pie pastry sheets)
- 2 pints fresh blueberries
- 1¼ cups granulated sugar
- 8 tablespoons (1 stick) unsalted butter, cut into pats
- ¼ cup water
- 1 teaspoon vanilla extract
- ½ teaspoon lemon extract
- Whipped cream or vanilla ice cream for serving

Preheat the oven to 350°F. Grease the sides of a 2-quart casserole dish and line the bottom and sides of the dish with 1 of the pieces of pie pastry. Place the remaining piece of pie pastry on a pastry cloth and set the casserole dish on top of it. Cut the pastry to fit the top of the casserole, leaving about 1 inch of pastry to overhang the dish on all sides. Set aside.

Carefully wash the blueberries and pick through and remove any remaining stems. Put half the blueberries in the bottom of the casserole dish. Sprinkle ½ cup of the sugar over them. Arrange ½ the butter pats on top of the blueberries. Pick up the cut away pieces of pie pastry that remain and place them on top of first layer of blueberries and butter. Layer the remaining berries, sugar, and butter in the same order overall.

In a liquid measuring cup, whisk together the water and vanilla and lemon extracts and pour the mixture over the top of the berries. Cover the cobbler with the oversized pastry and pinch together the edges to seal. Cut slits in the top of the crust to allow steam to escape. Bake for 1 hour. Remove from the oven. Allow to cool for 1 hour. Serve warm with whipped cream or vanilla ice cream on top.

Dessie's Peach Cobbler

I like to think that if Dessie were coming of age today, she'd be a child psychologist. She always knew how to make my brother George and me do just exactly what she wanted. She kept a fly swatter on top of the refrigerator, and that's what she "swatted" us with if we misbehaved. Dessie could wield that fly swatter with the grace that a fly fisherman casts his line—and make the accompanying swishing sounds to go with it. Just seeing her arm reaching toward the top of the refrigerator was usually enough to get us back in line. Dessie usually had an early warning system that we were about to get the fly swatter: she would say in her Lowcountry accent, "I ain't playing with you now," and one hand would go on her hip. If we didn't straighten up and the second hand made it on to her other hip, she was "two-hip serious," my brother George would say. That was when we really knew we were in trouble!

In retrospect, I don't think that in the few times the fly swatter was moved from its resting place, she ever landed many swats. She'd just let that anticipation build with that swishing sound and the fussing at you that went along with it. The bigger punishment was knowing you had disappointed her.

Sharon, a high-school friend of mine who grew up on St. Helena Island, also recalled being swatted with a fly swatter as a child. One day, her younger sister grew weary of such punishment and decided to take matters into her own hands. She absconded with the fly swatter and buried it in the back yard, but according to Sharon, "Alas, it was a shallow grave." Her mother went in search of the fly swatter, to no avail. Once she walked out into the back yard, though, she spotted the hopeful final resting place of the fly swatter—roughly the same shape and size of the fly swatter itself. With little difficulty, the fly swatter was retrieved and put to its prior use on her little sister's behind. I don't think any of us have ever used a fly swatter in our adulthood, in solidarity with the flies!

My mother's extended family grew peaches in the upstate of South Carolina. In the summertime, we'd make our way to Greer and for our return trip we'd load up the car with lots of fresh peaches to share with folks in Beaufort. The kitchen in the house we lived in back then had a counter-height square water heater just adjacent to the stove. Whenever we had fresh peaches, Dessie would make one of her fabulous peach cobblers and set it on top of that water heater to cool.

In the kitchen, we also had a metal trash can with a flip-up top. While the cobbler was cooling, my brother George would sneak into the kitchen, grab a spoon out of the drawer, pull the trash can over to the water heater, and stand on top of the trash can so he could eat the cobbler right out of the pan. Dessie would always go in and shoo him away—it was almost a game between the two of them.

One day, Dessie decided she was going to "fix him," to use her own words. That day, Dessie made TWO peach cobblers. She put one in its usual place and set the second one on top of the refrigerator to cool. Not once during that day did she go in the kitchen to shoo George away from the peach cobbler atop the water heater. He ended up eating so much of it that he got awfully sick and refused to touch peach cobbler again until he was grown—and when I say grown, I mean deep into his twenties. It suited me just fine, as peach was always my favorite anyway!

When George was growing up, he was very fastidious in his dress and a very picky eater, and Dessie catered to him with her cooking. In his late forties, George battled non-Hodgkin's lymphoma for several years. The morning he was slipping away, he drifted in and out of consciousness and was mostly incoherent when he talked. The one word I could clearly understand him saying was "Dessie." She'd been gone about five years by then, but I truly believe she had come to take him home to heaven. I'm also sure she had a peach cobbler ready for him.

Makes 8 to 10 servings

1 (14.1-ounce) box refrigerated pie crust (contains 2 pie pastry sheets)

1½ cups granulated sugar, divided

¼ cup all-purpose flour

¼ teaspoon freshly grated nutmeg

¼ teaspoon ground cinnamon

¼ teaspoon salt

8 to 10 peaches, peeled and sliced

8 tablespoons (1 stick) unsalted butter, cut into pats

Whipped cream or vanilla ice cream for serving

Preheat the oven to 375°F. Grease the sides of a 2-quart casserole dish and line the bottom and sides of the dish with 1 of the pieces of pie pastry. Place the remaining piece of pie pastry on a pastry cloth and set the casserole dish on top of it. Cut the pastry to fit the top of the casserole, leaving about 1 inch of pastry to overhang the dish on all sides. Set aside.

In a large bowl, mix 1¼ cups of the sugar with the flour, nutmeg, cinnamon, and salt. Add the peaches and toss until they are well coated.

Place half the peach mixture in the bottom of the casserole dish. Arrange half the butter pats on top of the peaches. Pick up the cut away pieces of pie pastry that remain and place them on top of first layer of peaches and butter. Layer the remaining peaches and butter in the same order over all.

Cover the cobbler with the oversized pastry and pinch together the edges to seal. Sprinkle the top with the remaining ¼ cup sugar. Cut slits in the top of the crust to allow steam to escape. Bake for 10 minutes. Reduce the oven temperature to 275°F and bake for 50 minutes more. Remove from the oven. Allow to cool for 1 hour, keeping little boys away from it. Serve warm with whipped cream or vanilla ice cream on top.

Huguenot Torte

I would love to be able to wax eloquently about how this dish was brought to the new world by Beaufort's founder, Jean Ribault, a French Huguenot looking for religious freedom, but sadly, that is not the case. It was originally from the Ozarks of Arkansas, and a Charleston housewife adapted it for the tavern she worked in during the Depression era of the 1930s; it was called, appropriately enough, the Huguenot Tavern.

The Huguenot Torte became one of the specialties of Robinson's Cafeteria, a locally owned cafeteria in Charleston. Robinson's was one of Aunt Mary's favorite places to eat and specifically to "get her vegetables," along with a little dessert at the end of the meal. This is how it came to be part of my family's repertoire.

Makes 6 to 8 servings

- 1 whole large egg
- ¾ cup granulated sugar
- 2 tablespoons all-purpose flour
- 1¼ teaspoons baking powder
- ⅛ teaspoon salt
- 1 teaspoon vanilla extract
- ½ cup chopped pecans plus more for sprinkling tops
- ½ cup tart cooking apples, such as Granny Smiths, chopped
- Whipped cream for serving

Preheat the oven to 325°F. Grease a 9-inch pie pan with butter or baking spray with flour.

Using a hand mixer or stand mixer on medium-high speed, beat the egg until light and frothy. Add the sugar and mix until creamed together.

In a separate bowl, sift together the flour, baking powder, and salt. Add the flour mixture to the egg mixture, beating until all the dry ingredients are well combined. Add the vanilla and mix well. Stir in the pecans and apples by hand.

Transfer the mixture to the prepared pie pan and bake until the top is golden brown and crusty, about 35 minutes. Remove from the oven and set aside to cool for a few minutes before serving.

To serve, use a large spatula to place a portion of the torte on a dessert plate. Top with the whipped cream and sprinkle a few pecans on top.

Hand Pies

My mother always used to talk about the fried hand pies my great-grandmother made, and I remember my grandmother making them, too. These half-moon shaped fried peach or apple turnovers were just the perfect size to fit in your hand. I searched through all the recipe boxes in the house, but the only recipe I could find for the hand pies was a very cryptic one: the filling called for a "peck of peaches, 8 cups of sugar, and 2 cups of vinegar." I thought that sounded a little harsh, so I played around with it until I came up with something that tasted like the ones I remembered. These are pretty darn close.

The filling can be made when the fresh fruit is in season and frozen, so you can put it to use when that fresh fruit is a distant memory. To make apple hand pies, substitute 2 cups of finely chopped Granny Smith or other cooking apples for the peaches. Cook the apples with the other filling ingredients in a saucepan for 30 to 45 minutes. The pies are easy to assemble using pre-made crusts, and the hand pies can also be frozen after assembly and baked later. It's a wonderfully sinful indulgence to have the leftovers for breakfast—if they don't become a midnight snack first!

Makes 20 pies

FILLING

2 cups peeled and chopped peaches (3 to 4 peaches)

¼ cup granulated sugar

¼ cup packed light brown sugar

2 teaspoons lemon juice

1 teaspoon apple cider vinegar

¼ teaspoon ground cinnamon

½ teaspoon vanilla extract

½ teaspoon almond extract

¼ teaspoon salt

1 tablespoon cornstarch dissolved in 1 tablespoon water

(*continued*)

Make the Filling: Combine peaches, sugars, lemon juice, vinegar, cinnamon, extracts, and salt in a heavy saucepan over medium heat and bring to a boil. Reduce the heat to medium to low, add the cornstarch slurry to the peach mixture, and cook for 10 minutes, until the mixture thickens. Remove from the heat and transfer the filling to a small bowl. Refrigerate for at least 2 hours. (The filling may also be frozen and then thawed completely before using.)

Make the Pies: Preheat the oven to 425°F. Line 2 large baking sheets with parchment paper or foil; if using foil, grease it with baking spray with flour.

Dust a pastry cloth or a clean countertop with flour. Remove 1 pie crust pastry sheet from its packaging, unroll it, and roll it out slightly using a rolling pin. Cut 4 (4-inch) circles out of the pastry. (A plastic lid makes a good 4-inch cutter.) Gather the pastry scraps into a

PIES

2 (14.1-ounce) boxes refrigerated pie crust (contains 4 pie pastry sheets total)

1 large egg white

1 teaspoon water

GLAZE

2½ cups confectioners' sugar

⅓ to ½ cup whole milk

ball, roll them out again, and cut a fifth (4-inch) circle. Place the circles of dough on the prepared baking sheets. Repeat with the remaining pastry sheets until you have 20 circles.

Place 1 heaping tablespoon of the pie filling in the center of each pie crust. Do not overfill, or the pies won't seal well. Wet the edges of half of each crust and fold the opposite side of the crust over the wet edge. Press with a fork to seal the edges. Arrange the pies about 1 inch apart on the baking sheets. (Unbaked pies can be wrapped and frozen at this point.)

Beat together the egg white and water in a small bowl. Using a pastry brush, brush the egg mixture over the top of each pie. Bake until golden brown, about 20 to 25 minutes. Remove from the oven. Transfer the pies to a wire rack and set aside to cool for 5 to 10 minutes.

Make the Glaze: While the pies are cooling, mix together the confectioners' sugar and milk in a shallow bowl. Dip the tops of the pies, one at a time, into the glaze. Return each of the pies to the wire rack and allow the glaze to dry. Serve warm.

Gran-Gran's Apple Cake

My grandmother was a devout Methodist. Her family helped to found several churches in the upstate of South Carolina, including Wood's Chapel near what is now the BMW plant and Memorial Methodist in Greer. Gran-Gran was a stickler for saying a blessing before meals, and this is the one she taught us as children. It is attributed to John Wesley, the father of Methodism, although it is now believed that it was written for him to use, and not written by him. Regardless of its author, it always hung on the wall of my grandmother's kitchen, and it still hangs in the Beaufort house's kitchen to this day.

Be present at our table, Lord.
Be here and everywhere adored.
All thy creatures bless,
And grant that we may feast in Paradise with thee. Amen.

If it hadn't been for that snake and his durned apple, we'd all be feasting every day in Paradise. Here's hoping this cake will make all your earthly meals seem like a feast in Paradise.

Makes 12 to 16 servings

CAKE

2 cups granulated sugar
1¼ cups vegetable oil
3 whole large eggs
1 tablespoon light rum
1 teaspoon almond extract
1 teaspoon vanilla extract
3 cups all-purpose flour
1 teaspoon baking soda
1 teaspoon salt
3 cups peeled diced apples plus 2 apples, peeled and very thinly sliced for top of cake

(*continued*)

Make the Cake: Preheat the oven to 350°F. Grease a 10-inch tube pan (not a Bundt pan) with butter and dust it with flour or use a baking spray with flour.

Using a hand mixer or stand mixer on medium speed, cream together the sugar, oil, eggs, rum, and extracts until well blended. In a separate bowl, sift together the flour, baking soda, and salt. Gradually add the flour mixture to the sugar mixture, mixing until well combined. Fold the diced apples, raisins, and nuts into the batter.

Arrange the sliced apples in a circle in the bottom of the prepared tube pan (meaning that when the cake is inverted, the apples will be on top). Pour the batter on top of the arranged apples. Bake until the top is golden brown and the cake springs back when poked, about 1 hour and 20 minutes. When the cake is done, remove from the oven and invert onto a cake plate. Set aside to cool slightly.

1 cup raisins

1 cup chopped nuts

ICING

1 cup packed light brown sugar

8 tablespoons (1 stick) unsalted butter

¼ cup evaporated milk

Make the Icing: Combine all of the ingredients in a saucepan over medium heat and bring to a boil. Boil for 2 minutes, stirring often. Remove from the heat and pour over the cake.

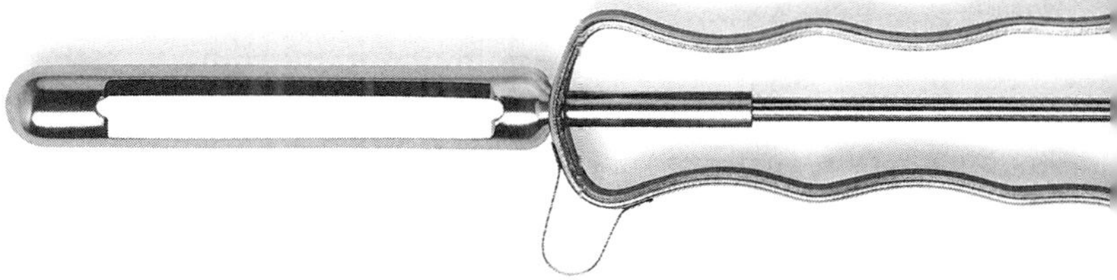

Grasshopper Pie

Grasshopper pie was one of the signature desserts served at the old Fort Sumter Hotel in Charleston. Before it was converted into condos in the 1980s, the hotel had an elegant restaurant called the Rampart Room that wrapped around the side that faced the harbor.

Now, I was a constant source of embarrassment to my mother as a child in that I was a something of a tomboy—and, as she used to say, "a blunderbuss." My brother George, being the eldest and the boy, was, of course, *the perfect* child in my mother's eyes. Except for one particular day at the Fort Sumter Hotel.

One day, my mother and Aunt Mimi took my older brother and me to Charleston to go shopping, followed by lunch in the Rampart Room. This was in the early sixties, when women really got dressed up to go shopping on King Street, so I'm sure Mother was dressed to the nines. I was a babe in arms, so I could not be somehow blamed for this episode. Mother was carrying me through the lobby of the Fort Sumter Hotel, smiling and nodding at people as she walked by, and George trailed behind her. Eventually, she noticed that people were smiling and nodding back a little more than usual, and almost . . . laughing.

George and me, Easter 1964, at my grandmother's house in Greer, before they moved to Beaufort. Notice my lovely posture.

Mother turned around to find my "perfect" six-year-old brother walking behind her like Quasimodo, with one arm pulled up to his face and dragging his other foot along behind him. George also had contorted his face—as Mother said, "just like Mortimer Snerd," a rather dimwitted dummy used by the famous ventriloquist Edgar Bergen. I am sure my mother was "Mort-ti-fied." George got a knot jerked in him in the bathroom of the Fort Sumter, and I'm not even sure we ate lunch there that day. But I do know that George Greene never lived that down in my mother's eyes, and she told that story every time we went to or by the Fort Sumter Hotel, even for many years after it closed.

Every time I make this grasshopper pie, I think about Mother, George, Mortimer Snerd, and lots of happy lunches at the old Fort Sumter Hotel.

Makes 6 to 8 servings

14 chocolate sandwich cookies

2 tablespoons unsalted butter, softened

24 regular marshmallows

½ cup whole milk

¼ cup green crème de menthe liqueur

2 tablespoons crème de cacao liqueur

1 cup whipping cream

Whipped cream and chocolate syrup for serving

Grease a 9-inch glass pie dish with butter.

Crush the cookies into the bowl of a food processor. Add the butter and pulse until blended. Press the mixture into the bottom and sides of the pie dish and set aside.

Combine the marshmallows and milk in the top of a double boiler and warm until the mixture is completely melted and smooth. Remove from the heat and set aside to cool. Add the crème de menthe and crème de cacao and stir until smooth.

In a separate bowl, using a hand mixer or stand mixer on high speed, beat the whipping cream until stiff. Fold the whipped cream into the marshmallow mixture until well blended.

Transfer the mixture into the prepared pie dish and spread it evenly. Freeze the pie for several hours or overnight; the pie can be made ahead and kept in the freezer for several weeks.

Serve frozen with a dollop of whipped cream and a drizzle of chocolate syrup on top.

Chocolate Bourbon Pecan Pie

My mother always made beautiful candy plates to give to friends for Christmas presents. Most of the candy required use of a thermometer and boiling it to a certain temperature, which meant it was highly subject to the humidity of the Lowcountry. One year, about the time Mother got out of school for Christmas break and was about to begin her candy making, rain set in for several days—not just rain, but a veritable monsoon.

This recipe, which is officially named after a famous horse race in Kentucky, had been given to Mother by a friend, so she decided to make these pies to give for Christmas presents instead. We gave them to several of our Baptist friends, including the preacher and his wife. After Christmas, the wife asked for the recipe. Mother didn't want to list the bourbon as one of the ingredients, so she just wrote "flavoring" and dispatched my brother over with the recipe and the flavoring in a small jar.

I am sure the preacher's wife knew exactly what the flavoring was, but it was never discussed between them. I understand that the real name of this pie has been copyrighted by the horse race, and it's not supposed to be used anywhere without their permission—so we'll just refer to it as The Preacher's Wife's Pie.

Makes 6 to 8 servings

1 cup pecan halves

2 whole large eggs

½ cup packed light brown sugar

½ cup granulated sugar

½ cup all-purpose flour

½ cup (1 stick) unsalted butter, melted

3 to 4 tablespoons bourbon (used for "flavoring")

1 teaspoon vanilla extract

½ teaspoon salt

1 cup semi-sweet chocolate chips

1 (9-inch) deep-dish pie shell, unbaked

Whipped cream for serving

Preheat the oven to 350°F.

Spread the pecans on a rimmed baking sheet and toast for 8 to 10 minutes. Reserve a few of the best halves for garnish and chop the remaining pecans into large pieces. Set aside.

In a large bowl, lightly beat the eggs. Add the sugars, flour, butter, bourbon, vanilla, and salt and stir until well combined.

Place the chocolate chips in a microwave-safe bowl and heat on high for 1½ to 2 minutes, depending on the wattage of your microwave. Remove from the microwave and stir until the chocolate is completely melted. Add the chocolate and chopped pecans to the filling mixture and stir well.

Spread the filling mixture into the pie shell and place the reserved pecan halves on top. Bake until done, 45 to 50 minutes. Remove from the oven, allow to cool for 1 to 2 hours to room temperature and serve with whipped cream on top.

NOTE: This recipe can also be baked in 12 (3-inch) tart shells. Bake until done, 30 to 40 minutes.

Gold Eagle Benne Seed Delight with Benne Wafers

This recipe is from the old Gold Eagle Hotel in Beaufort, which was an elegant inn built in Beaufort during the 1930s and torn down in the early 1960s. The owner and developer, Kate Gleason, envisioned Beaufort as a recreational retreat for wealthy visitors. She is widely credited with building the first golf course in Beaufort County. In the Gold Eagle's heyday, it welcomed such luminaries as Clark Gable, Somerset Maugham, and Adlai Stevenson. Her vision of Beaufort as a resort community would be recognized one day, but Kate was just about forty years ahead of her time.

This sauce recipe belonged to the daughter of the next owners of the Gold Eagle, Mrs. Dreka Stokes, a friend of my grandmother's. It makes an excellent Christmas present or hostess gift. Store the sauce in individual jars after cooking and tie a small bag of toasted benne seeds to the jar with a decorative ribbon. For an extra special gift, add a tin of Benne Cookies (see recipe below) and a gift certificate for some ice cream.

Makes 1 quart or 16 (¼-cup) servings

3½ cups packed light brown sugar

1 cup evaporated milk

1 cup miniature marshmallows

½ cup unsalted butter

1 teaspoon vanilla extract

Vanilla ice cream for serving

½ cup benne seeds, toasted (see note)

Combine the brown sugar, evaporated milk, marshmallows, butter, and vanilla in the top of a double boiler over medium heat and warm, stirring often, until the mixture is completely melted and smooth. Remove from the heat.

Transfer to lidded jars and store in the refrigerator. Reheat the sauce in the microwave as needed and serve warm over good-quality vanilla ice cream with toasted benne seeds sprinkled over the top.

Note: Line a baking sheet with sides with foil. Spread the seeds in a thin layer on the prepared baking sheet and bake in a 375°F oven until the seeds are turning golden brown, about 10 minutes. Shake the pan occasionally during baking to make sure the seeds do not burn. Benne seeds, which are a kind of sesame seed, can now be ordered from Anson Mills in Columbia at www.ansonmills.com.

BENNE SEED COOKIES

Benne (rhymes with penny) is the Gullah word for seed; these seeds are said to bring good luck. Some brides in the Lowcountry serve these cookies at their weddings to bless their marriage.

Makes 5 dozen

- 1½ cups packed light brown sugar
- ¾ cup unsalted butter, room temperature
- 1 whole large egg
- 1 cup all-purpose flour, sifted
- ¼ teaspoon baking soda
- 1 teaspoon vanilla extract
- 1 cup benne seeds, toasted

Preheat the oven to 325°F. Line 2 or more baking sheets with parchment paper and lightly butter paper.

Using a hand mixer or stand mixer on medium-high speed, cream together the brown sugar and butter. Reduce speed to medium and add egg, beating until it is creamed with the butter mixture. Add the remaining ingredients in order and mix.

Using a #110 scoop, a ½ teaspoon measure, or a small teaspoon, drop portions of the dough 2 inches apart onto the prepared baking sheets; the cookies will spread a lot. Bake until lightly golden brown, 10 to 12 minutes. Remove from the oven and set aside to cool for 5 minutes on the baking sheets. Transfer to wire racks to cool completely. Serve or store in an airtight container for up to 1 to 2 days. They are very susceptible to humidity and will not stay crisp long.

Key Lime Pie

After Aunt Mimi died, a wonderful woman named Barbara Walker came to help take care of Aunt Mary and my mother. Barbara was a godsend to all of us during that time. One weekend, I was cooking supper while Barbara helped Mary Dob eat some mushed-up chicken and rice, which was all she was able to swallow at that point. I then fixed Aunt Mary some dessert—homemade angel food cake with mashed fresh strawberries and whipped cream—and Barbara helped her eat it.

Once I finished making supper for the rest of us, Mother, Barbara, and I sat down to eat. When we finished eating, I fixed some dessert for us.

Aunt Mary looked at me and said, "Aren't you going to fix *me* any dessert?" I replied that she'd already eaten her dessert.

"I have NOT!" she exclaimed. I figured that since she was ninety-six years old, I really shouldn't argue with her. If she wanted to pretend that she hadn't had dessert, that was fine: it wasn't going to make any difference if she had another. I think that the rest of us shouldn't wait until we're ninety-six to try that trick—go for it now!

This refreshing pie, a summertime classic, is so light that you *could* eat dessert twice in the same sitting. Key limes are smaller limes that are paler than the large Persian limes typically found in grocery stores. If Key limes aren't available, look for authentic Key lime juice in the beverage section of the grocery store.

The filling for this recipe can also be used with the graham cracker tart shells that are commercially made by those fabulous little elves; they're available in the baking section of most grocery stores. These tarts are an easy dessert that can be kept in the freezer and pulled out individually as a cool treat for company.

Makes 6 to 8 servings

1 (5½-ounce) package chocolate-covered graham crackers

3 tablespoons unsalted butter, softened

2 large eggs, separated

1 (15-ounce) can sweetened condensed milk

⅔ cup freshly squeezed Key lime juice (5 to 6 Key limes)

1 tablespoon freshly grated lime zest

Few drops green food coloring (optional)

⅓ cup granulated sugar

Whipped cream and chocolate syrup for serving

Grease a 9-inch glass pie dish with butter.

Break up the crackers by hand into the bowl of a food processor. Add the butter and process until well blended. Press the mixture into the prepared dish.

Whisk the egg yolks in a medium bowl until they are thick. Add the condensed milk, lime juice, and lime zest and continue whisking until well blended. Add the food coloring, if desired, but only until the mixture turns a pale green color.

Using a hand mixer or stand mixer on high speed, beat the egg whites until stiff but not dry. While continuing to run the mixer, add the sugar in a gradual stream until the mixture becomes very stiff. Fold the egg white mixture into the lime mixture.

Pour the filling into the pie crust and freeze until firm, at least 6 hours. Serve topped with the whipped cream and drizzled with chocolate syrup.

Lemon Cheesecake

This is everyone's favorite cheesecake. Even folks who say, "I don't like cheesecake," love the creamy texture that mascarpone cheese adds to this delicious dessert. I make several of them each year to give as Christmas presents, some of which are presented drawn and quartered—no, not some medieval form of torture, but cut into four sections and wrapped individually so that the sections can be frozen, pulled out when needed, and served more easily.

The cake is delicious as is, but for an extra-special occasion, layer some fresh peach slices in a circular pattern on top of the cheesecake, and drizzle the topping from the Peach Delight dessert (p. 203) over and between the peaches; be sure to also allow the topping to drizzle down the sides of the cake. For a variation, try fresh peaches and raspberry Jell-O for a peach Melba flavor, or layer with fresh strawberries on top and use strawberry Jell-O for the topping. My brother George also liked it with a dollop of blueberry pie filling. Topping with fresh fruit makes it a beautiful summertime treat!

Makes 12 to 16 servings

SHORTBREAD CRUST

15 pecan shortbread cookies (yields about ½ cup finely ground)

½ cup unsalted butter (1 stick), at room temperature

½ cup all-purpose flour

¼ cup granulated sugar

CHEESECAKE

4 (8-ounce) packages cream cheese, softened

1 (8-ounce) container mascarpone cheese

(*continued*)

Make the Crust: Preheat the oven to 350°F. Line the bottom of a 9-inch springform pan with foil and then assemble the pan. Grease the foil and the sides of the pan with butter or baking spray with flour.

Break up the cookies into fourths and place them in the bowl of a food processor. Process into fine crumbs. Add the butter, flour, and sugar and process until all of the ingredients are blended together. Press the mixture evenly into the bottom of the pan.

Tear off 2 sheets of foil and stack one on top of the other, turning one so that together, they form an 8-point star. Set the springform pan in the center of the foil star and roll the foil around the pan, forming a collar that will prevent the butter in the crust from baking out of the bottom of the pan. Bake until the crust is golden brown, 20 to 25 minutes. Remove from the oven and set aside to cool, leaving the pan in the foil collar; leave the oven on.

- 1½ cups granulated sugar
- 2 whole large eggs
- 3 tablespoons freshly squeezed lemon juice
- Freshly grated zest of 1 large lemon
- 1 teaspoon lemon extract

Make the Cheesecake: Using a hand mixer or stand mixer on medium-high speed, beat together the cream cheese and mascarpone cheese until smooth and fluffy. Continuing to beat the mixture on medium speed, add the sugar and then beat in the eggs one at a time. Beat in the lemon juice, zest, and extract.

Turn off the mixer and pour the mixture into the cooled crust. Set the cheesecake pan, still in its foil collar, into a roasting pan. Fill the roasting pan with 1 inch of very hot water. Bake on the center rack of the oven until the cake is set and the top just begins to brown, about 1 hour. Remove the springform pan from the roasting pan and the foil collar. Set it aside to cool slightly on a wire rack.

Refrigerate for 6 hours or overnight.

When the cake is completely cooled, run a knife around the side of the pan. Unlock the pan and remove the sides. Carefully peel away the foil from the bottom section of the pan and then from the cake's crust. Place on a serving plate and serve with toppings as desired.

The "Momma" Cake or Easter Lemon Coconut Cake

This cake is a tribute to three very important women. While we'd made pieces and parts of this cake for years, my mother and I put them all together for an Easter brunch in Columbia many years ago. The divinity icing recipe is hers, and I wish that I'd paid more attention back then so I'd know exactly how she made it. I've had to go back and experiment on my own to figure it out.

The layers are Mrs. Kitty Windham's lemon pound cake, and the lemon filling is the recipe of the mother of Senator J. Verne Smith, Sr., one of the longest serving state senators in South Carolina. He referred to his wife, Jean, as "Momma," so this is the Momma Cake.

J. Verne, as he was known, was famous for folksy sayings like, "there's no education in the second kick of a mule," and for being a longtime advocate for, as he referred to them, "the frail elderly and raggedy-ass children." When lobbyists brought clients to see him and toted along large briefing notebooks, he was known to say, "I'm not much on notebooks. If you can't explain it to me in two sentences, don't bother." He once looked at a much younger fellow senator and asked, "Senator, you reckon you can tell that to the committee a'gin, a little slower, and without all that flowery language?" Ever a fan of slow, deliberate speech, it is said he once told a lobbyist, "Ma'am, you're talkin' faster than I can listen."

Mother holding me with George at her side as we dye Easter eggs in spring 1960 using my mother's Napoleon Ivy Wedgwood China. I am sure each and every one of George's eggs were immaculate, as everything he did was always perfect. I don't look too sure about the whole process.

J. Verne was known as a great storyteller, particularly during long Senate filibusters. One of his most notorious stories involved the *zuzu* flies. Many years ago, a farmer named Quillen Luellen worked for J. Verne's momma on the family's peach farm. A South Carolina highway patrolman once stopped Quillen for driving a peach flat on the highway that should have only been driven on the farm. While they were stopped on the side of the road, flies swarmed all around the officer as he questioned Quillen as to why he was driving the flat on the highway. As the officer swatted at the flies, Quillen identified the insects as *zuzu* flies.

The officer asked how Quillen knew exactly what kind of flies they were. Quillen replied that they were the kind of flies that flew around the "south end of a north-bound mule" when he was plowing. This did not sit well with the officer, who asked Quillen if he was saying the officer was a mule's ass.

Quillen said, "No, *I'm* not saying that, but it is awfully hard to fool a *zuzu* fly!"

According to J. Verne's son Jeff, telling the whole story in much elaborate detail takes at least ten minutes. After he would entertain the Senate with the story, J. Verne would somehow relate it to the issue at hand, and if you weren't in total agreement with whatever side he was supporting, you just might be referred to as something that would attract a *zuzu* fly.

Mother used this icing recipe not only for icing but also to make divinity candy when cooked to a higher temperature (252°F). Divinity icing can be tricky to make; this recipe doesn't work well when it is raining or otherwise very humid. It also sets up very quickly, so you must move rapidly when icing the cake. You can always go back later and smooth things out by dipping a knife into warm water and running it over the icing. If you don't want to attempt the divinity icing, or if a monsoon sets in when you need to make this cake, use the cream cheese frosting from the Carrot Cake recipe (p. 173), but reduce the amount of milk to 2 tablespoons and add 1 tablespoon freshly squeezed lemon juice and 1 teaspoon finely grated lemon zest.

Makes 16 servings

1 recipe Miss Kitty's Lemon Pound Cake, baked into 3 (10-inch) layers (p. 200)

LEMON FILLING (SEE NOTES)

3 whole large eggs

1 cup granulated sugar

1 tablespoon freshly squeezed lemon juice

1 teaspoon finely grated lemon zest

4 slices white bread

2 tablespoons unsalted butter

DIVINITY ICING

2½ cups granulated sugar

½ cup light corn syrup

½ cup water

2 large egg whites at room temperature (see notes)

½ teaspoon cream of tartar

1 teaspoon vanilla extract

4 cups freshly grated coconut

Make the Cake: Bake the layers in 3 (10-inch) round greased pans until a skewer inserted in the centers of the layers comes out clean, 45 to 50 minutes. Remove from the oven and set aside to cool completely.

Make the Filling: Beat the eggs in a medium bowl until they are a creamy yellow. Stir in the sugar, lemon juice, and lemon zest. Transfer the contents of the bowl to the top of a double boiler.

Trim the crusts from the bread. Place 1 piece of the bread under running water until it is wet and then squeeze the water from the bread. Crumble the moistened bread into the top of the double boiler and repeat with the remaining pieces of bread. Whisk the mixture until the bread dissolves and cook for about 10 minutes, until the mixture thickens. Add the butter and stir until the butter is melted. Remove from the heat.

While the mixture is still warm, beat it with a whisk until it is smooth and air is incorporated.

Spread the warm lemon filling on the top of the bottom cake layer. Add the second layer and an additional coating of filling and place the top layer on the filling. Set the cake aside until the filling sets and will hold the layers together.

Make the Icing: In a large saucepan over medium heat, combine the sugar, corn syrup, and water and bring to a boil. Boil until a little of the mixture dropped in cold water forms into a firm ball (once the mixture reaches, 246°F to 250°F measured with a candy thermometer). Remove from the heat.

Using a hand mixer or stand mixer on high speed, beat the egg whites until they are foamy. Add the cream of tartar and continue beating until the egg whites are very stiff. With the mixer still running, pour the warm sugar mixture into the egg whites in a slow, steady stream. Add the vanilla and beat for 7 to 10 minutes, until the icing holds together well and is not runny; it will cool significantly while it is being beaten. It is ready when a spoonful dropped on a piece of wax paper stays in a mound and does not spread.

Quickly ice the cake with the divinity icing and then press the grated coconut into the sides and edges of the cake before the icing sets completely. Serve.

NOTES: If you want a thicker layer of lemon filling, double the recipe. It can be kept in refrigerator for up to 1 week. The filling can also be used to make 1 (9-inch) pie or 8 tarts. If you choose to make the tarts, they're wonderful topped with the meringue from the Soul-Satisfying Chocolate Meringue Pie recipe (p. 172). Fill a pastry bag with the meringue and pipe it on to the tarts in a circular motion, building higher toward the center. Bake the tarts with the meringue according to the directions in the chocolate pie recipe.

If you forget to bring your eggs to room temperature, place them in a bowl of warm water a few minutes prior to separating them and beating the egg whites. It really makes a difference in terms of the volume you can achieve.

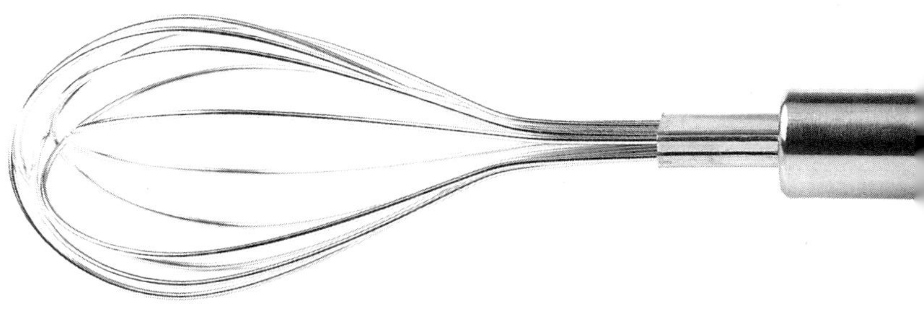

Miss Kitty's Lemon Pound Cake

This is the signature dessert of my best friend Jane's mother, Kathryn Huntley Windham, otherwise known as Kitty. To our generation, she was known as Miss Kitty. The original recipe was given to her eldest daughter, Cindy Windham Duryea, at a dessert shower before she married in 1974. The lady who gave her the recipe was "Mamma T," a Mrs. Talbert from their hometown of Aiken, South Carolina. Mamma T told Cindy, "Honey, if you learn to make this, you won't ever have to learn to make another dessert." My, how right she was!

The first time I remember having it was when I visited the Windhams when Jane and I were in college, and I've been making it ever since. If anyone passes away, I always bring the family a lemon pound cake.

On the morning Mrs. Windham passed away, November 1, she called their back-door neighbor, who was a nurse. She told her, "I don't feel well. I think I ate too much Halloween candy."

In fact, Miss Kitty was having a heart attack. Though she made it to the hospital, she passed away shortly after Jane and Cindy arrived. Later in the day, Jane sent me a picture of the wastepaper basket beside her mother's chair. It contained many miniature Halloween candy wrappers and the foil wrappers from two Klondike bars. That's not what killed her, but according to Jane, she had, in fact, eaten too much Halloween candy. We all like to say that when it's our time to go, we want it to be on November 1 and for it to be from thinking we ate too much Halloween candy.

The Windhams were also longtime University of South Carolina Gamecock fans—season-ticketholders in multiple sports over many years. The year Mrs. Windham died was also her youngest grandchild Sally's senior year of high school. On Christmas Eve of that year, when Jane's family returned from church, Sally pulled a *huge* envelope that read "You are Tigertown bound" from the mailbox. It contained her early acceptance letter to Clemson University—the in-state school whose teams were the Gamecocks' archrivals. Jane told Sally it was a good thing her grandmother was already dead from eating too much Halloween candy because she'd have had a stroke right there on the front porch on Christmas Eve at the thought of her youngest grandchild going to Clemson! But Sally had a wonderful time at Clemson, and we've all tried hard to root for the Tigers too, especially during their runs at the national football championship. But I'm not sure Miss Kitty could ever have brought herself to do that . . .

Miss Kitty always baked this cake in a long 5 × 16-inch loaf pan. They are available online from the Wilton Company. This pan makes the cake extremely easy to slice.

At a luncheon I attended in Beaufort, I brought along one of Miss Kitty's pound cakes baked in that long pan. A lady attending the luncheon looked around and asked, "Is Cindy Duryea here?" I replied, "No, but that's her momma's pound cake recipe." That's how much this cake and that pan are associated with the Windham and Duryea families.

Makes 20 servings

CAKE

3 cups granulated sugar

1 cup (2 sticks) unsalted butter

½ cup butter-flavored vegetable shortening

6 whole large eggs

1 tablespoon lemon extract

3½ cups all-purpose flour

1 teaspoon baking powder

½ teaspoon salt

1 cup whole milk

GLAZE

6 tablespoons unsalted butter, melted

3 tablespoons lemon juice

2 cups confectioners' sugar, sifted

Make the Cake: Preheat the oven to 300°F. Grease a 5 × 16-inch loaf pan with butter and dust it with flour or use a baking spray with flour. (For other pans, see below.)

Using a hand mixer or stand mixer on high speed, cream together the sugar, butter, and shortening. Add the eggs one at a time, beating well after each addition. Add the lemon extract and mix will.

In a separate bowl, sift together the flour, baking powder, and salt. Alternate adding the flour mixture (about a cup at a time) and the milk (about a third of a cup at a time) to the sugar-egg mixture until all of each is added, beginning and ending with the flour mixture. After each addition, scrape sides with a spatula and mix well. Pour the batter into the prepared pan.

If you are using a long loaf pan, bake until a toothpick or wooden skewer inserted into the center of the cake comes out clean, about 1 hour 25 minutes. For other sizes, adjust the time according to the chart below. Remove from the oven and set the cake aside in the pan for 20 minutes on a wire rack. Turn the cooled cake out of the pan and onto a cake board or a serving dish lined with wax paper. (I find that political yard signs saved after election day, wiped clean, cut to size, and covered in foil are perfect for this size of cake!)

Make the Glaze: While the cake is still warm, mix together the butter and lemon juice. Add the confectioner's sugar and mix well. Spoon the glaze over the cake and allow to set for at least 30 minutes. Serve.

OTHER PAN SIZES	BAKING TIME
Tube pan (not a Bundt pan)	1 hour 30 minutes
Long (5 × 16-inch) loaf pan	1 hour 25 minutes
2 (5 × 9-inch) loaf pans	1 hour 10 minutes
3 (2 × 4-inch) individual-well brownie pans	30 minutes

Peach Delight

My mother's extended family and a lot of her kinfolk in the Upstate of South Carolina always grew peaches. They talked about peaches the way Bubba Blue talked about shrimp in *Forrest Gump*—peach cobbler, peach ice cream, peach daiquiris, peach preserves, peach chutney, peach bread, peach hand pies. You name it, we made it out of peaches. This recipe was a summer favorite of my mother and aunts. The peaches and glaze also make a beautiful topping for the Lemon Cheesecake (p. 194), if you want to be extra fancy.

Makes 12 to 16 servings

FIRST LAYER, CRUST

½ cup unsalted butter, melted

2 cups all-purpose flour

1½ cups chopped pecans

SECOND LAYER, CREAM

2 (8-ounce) packages cream cheese, softened

2½ cups confectioners' sugar

2 cups Cool Whip non-dairy whipped topping

THIRD LAYER, PEACHES

6 to 8 peeled and sliced peaches

FOURTH LAYER, TOPPING

¼ cup self-rising flour

¼ cup peach-flavored powdered gelatin

1 cup granulated sugar

1 cup water

Make the Crust: Preheat the oven to 350°F. Grease a 9 × 13-inch ovenproof glass baking dish with butter.

Place the butter in a medium microwave-safe bowl and heat on high for 1 to 1½ minutes, depending on the wattage of your microwave, until melted. Add the flour and stir until smooth. Add the pecans and stir until they are well blended into the batter. Spread the batter in the bottom of the baking dish. Bake for 12 minutes. Remove from the oven and set aside to cool completely.

Make the Second Layer: Using a hand mixer or stand mixer on high speed, whip the cream cheese until it is light and fluffy. Add the confectioners' sugar and beat until it is blended with the cream cheese. Fold in the Cool Whip by hand with a spatula. Spread the cream layer over the cooled crust.

Make the Third Layer: Slice enough peaches to completely cover cream cheese mixture. Arrange in rows.

Make the Fourth Layer: Combine all of the ingredients in a saucepan over low heat and mix well. Cook, stirring until the flour and gelatin are dissolved, for 5 to 10 minutes. The mixture should thicken and become translucent. Remove from the heat.

Spoon the topping over the peaches, making sure each slice is well coated. Refrigerate for 6 hours or overnight. Slice into squares and serve cold.

Pecan Tarts

These tarts were introduced to us by our friend The Duhés, who hails from New Orleans, Louisiana. While we typically say "pee-can" in South Carolina, they say "pah-kahn" in Louisiana. No matter—they are delicious, however you pronounce them. I sent some of these tarts to friends in Maryland one year for Christmas and included a note that said, "The original recipe calls for topping them with whipped cream or ice cream." Bill dutifully complied and told his wife, "Mary said they *had* to be eaten this way." Enjoy!

Makes 12 tarts

- 12 ready-made frozen pastry tart shells (Dutch Anne brand is an option)
- 1 cup packed light brown sugar
- 2 tablespoons all-purpose flour
- 1 cup light corn syrup
- 1 tablespoon unsalted butter, melted
- 3 whole large eggs
- 1 teaspoon vanilla extract
- ¼ teaspoon salt
- 2 cups pecan halves
- Whipped cream or vanilla or butter pecan ice cream for serving

Preheat the oven to 325°F. Unwrap the tart shells and place them on a baking sheet with sides.

In a large bowl, stir together the brown sugar and flour. Add the corn syrup and butter and mix until blended.

In a separate bowl, beat the eggs. Add the vanilla and salt and beat until combined. Pour the egg mixture into the sugar mixture and stir until well blended. Add the pecans and stir until the pecans are well coated by the sugar mixture.

Using a #16 scoop or a ¼-cup measure, fill each of the tart shells with an equal amount of the filling. Bake 35 to 40 minutes until the tarts are set and golden brown. Remove from the oven and set aside to cool.

Serve topped with whipped cream or ice cream.

NOTE: These tarts freeze very well. Wrap them individually in plastic wrap and then store them in the freezer in ziplock bags. The night before you plan to use them, thaw as many as you need. The filling can also be baked into a 9-inch deep-dish pie shell for 1 hour at 325°F.

Wampee Pound Cake with Black Tea Ice Cream

Wampee is a conference center owned by Santee-Cooper, the state-owned utility company in South Carolina. The main house is an eighteenth-century home that was moved to its present site during the construction of a series of dams, during which its previous location and nearby areas were flooded and turned into lakes so the dams could generate power for rural areas in the 1930s.

The house is said to be haunted by ghosts who made the journey to the home's new location. One former Santee-Cooper board member who slept in the house claimed to have awoken in the middle of the night to find a face hovering over him in the bed. The next morning, he told the caretaker he'd resign from the board before he'd ever spend another night in that house. When I served on the State Deferred Compensation Commission, I was always glad to be assigned to one of the cottages and relieved that I'd never be important enough to sleep in the big house!

The best part of conferences at Wampee is the food. After consuming a *huge* breakfast, we always walked into our meetings swearing that we wouldn't eat for days—only to be greeted by a still-warm pound cake wrapped in a tea towel. How could you *not* have a piece while it was still warm? To decline a piece would have been rude to the wonderful ladies in the kitchen.

Makes 16 servings

- 1½ cups (3 sticks) unsalted butter, at room temperature
- 1 (8-ounce) package cream cheese, at room temperature
- 3 cups granulated sugar
- 6 whole large eggs
- 1 tablespoon vanilla extract
- 1 teaspoon almond extract
- 2 cups all-purpose flour
- 1 cup self-rising flour (see note)
- Black Tea Ice Cream for serving (optional; recipe follows)

Preheat the oven to 350°F. Grease a tube (not a Bundt) pan with butter and dust it with flour or use a baking spray with flour.

Using a hand mixer or stand mixer on high speed, cream together the butter and cream cheese for about 2 minutes, until the mixture is smooth and creamy. As the mixer continues to run on medium-to-high speed, add the sugar, ½ cup at a time, and continue to beat until the sugar is mostly dissolved. Add the eggs one at a time, beating well after each addition. Add the extracts and continue to mix until they are fully blended into the batter.

In a separate bowl, sift the flours together. Add the mixed flours, ½ cup at a time, to the batter. After each addition, mix well, using a rubber spatula to scrape down the sides and bottom to make sure all of the dry ingredients are fully incorporated into the batter.

Pour the batter into the prepared pan and tap the pan on the countertop a few times to remove any air pockets. Bake until a toothpick or wooden skewer inserted into the center of the cake comes out clean, about 1 hour and 15 minutes. Remove from the oven and set the cake aside in the pan for 20 minutes on a wire rack.

Turn the cooled cake out of the pan and onto a cake round or a serving dish lined with wax paper. If you are serving the cake immediately, wrap it in a clean tea towel to keep it warm. Serve topped with the Black Tea Ice Cream, if desired.

Note: To make your own self-rising flour, sift together 1 cup all-purpose flour, 1 teaspoon baking powder, and ½ teaspoon salt

BLACK TEA ICE CREAM

My friend Kim Morgan is a very talented genealogist and researcher. Among her many accomplishments is her work on the PBS television show *Finding Your Roots.* She came across this recipe in a 1920s newspaper and shared it with me—it's the perfect accompaniment for a slice of Wampee pound cake. Afterall, what's more Southern than sweet tea?

I have adjusted the directions from the original recipe, as I think many recipes of that era assumed a level of cooking skills that are not always present in today's world.

Makes 12 (½-cup) servings

3 large egg yolks

2 cups evaporated milk (see note)

1 cup water

1½ cups granulated sugar

6 black tea bags or 3 tablespoons black loose-leaf tea in a metal mesh tea ball

6 cloves

1 cup heavy cream

¼ cup freshly squeezed lemon juice

Freshly grated zest of 1 lemon

¼ teaspoon salt

Beat the egg yolks in a medium mixing bowl and set aside.

Combine 1 cup of the evaporated milk, the water, and the sugar in a medium saucepan over medium-to-low heat and cook until small bubbles form and steam starts to rise, but before it comes to a full boil (the temperature should be about 180°F). Add the tea bags and cloves, remove from the heat, and set aside to steep for 3 minutes, stirring occasionally. Remove the tea bags and squeeze them over the pan to remove any milk and extra tea flavor from the bags. Using a fine sieve, strain the contents of the saucepan into a bowl; remove and discard any extra tea leaves and the cloves.

Add about ½ cup of the hot milk to the egg yolks and beat the mixture well with a whisk; this will temper the egg yolks so they do not cook in the hot milk mixture. Repeat the process with a second ½ cup of the hot milk and then pour the tempered egg yolk mixture into the saucepan. Add the remaining 1 cup evaporated milk and the cream, stir, and return to low-to-medium heat. Cook for 5 to 10 minutes, until the mixture is thickened and will coat the back of a spoon. Stir in lemon juice, lemon zest, and salt and refrigerate until the mixture cools completely.

Place the mixture in an ice cream churn and freeze according to the manufacturer's directions. Transfer the ice cream to a freezer-safe container and allow to cure for 2 hours until completely frozen. Serve frozen.

NOTE: Since this recipe is from the 1920s, when pasteurized milk was not always readily available, it calls for a mixture of evaporated milk and water. If you prefer, you can substitute 3 cups of half-and-half for the evaporated milk and water. However, I recommend using evaporated milk, as it lends the ice cream a caramel flavor due to the process of making evaporated milk.

Aunt Lou's Famous Chocolate Roll

Remember Aunt Lou's Quick Shrimp Curry (p. 136) and her mini-bottle Easter egg hunt? She could fill a whole book of stories and recipes in and of herself. For example, whenever my older brother and I visited her as children, her idea of a bedtime story was an awful, scary ghost story about the house she lived in, which had been built in 1850—the very house in which we were staying. Then she'd kiss us good night and expect us to be able to sleep!

Perhaps Aunt Lou was best known for her chocolate rolls. When she passed away, the minister gave a beautiful eulogy. He claimed that he could stand up there and tell Lou stories all day long, but we'd all known her longer and probably had better stories than he did. (Which was true!) He then went on to share how Lou did a lot of things for people that others never knew about, like the fact that whenever someone was sick, she'd always take them a pot of her vegetable soup. And whenever someone lost a family member, he said, "she'd always take them one of her . . ." Before he could get the words out of his mouth, a whispered murmur of "chocolate rolls" swept across the congregation. Aunt Lou always kept a couple in the freezer and would send one back home with us whenever we visited.

Lou's recipe called for "uncooked" chocolate icing, but since it wasn't described further in the recipe, I assume it was something everyone knew how to make back in the 1950s. I had to go in search of one, but given the notes my mother wrote on Lou's recipe, I think what I've included here is pretty close.

Makes 8 to 10 servings

CAKE

- 6 large eggs, separated
- 1 teaspoon vanilla extract
- 1 cup confectioners' sugar plus more for sifting on tea towel
- ¼ cup unsweetened cocoa powder
- ¾ cup chopped pecans
- 1 cup whipping cream, whipped

Make the Cake: Preheat the oven to 325°F. Grease a 11 × 15-inch baking sheet with sides (also known as a jelly roll pan) with butter and then line the pan with wax or parchment paper. Grease the paper with butter and dust it with flour. Set aside.

Using a hand mixer or stand mixer on high speed, beat the egg whites until they are very stiff and peaks form and stay in place.

In a separate bowl, beat the egg yolks until they thicken. Add the vanilla to the yolks and stir until combined.

"UNCOOKED" CHOCOLATE ICING

1½ cups confectioners' sugar

¼ cup unsweetened cocoa powder

2 tablespoons whole milk

4 tablespoons (½ stick) unsalted butter, softened

½ teaspoon vanilla extract

In a separate bowl, sift together the 1 cup confectioners' sugar and the cocoa powder. Add the sugar mixture to the egg yolks and stir well (the mixture will be very thick). Fold the sugar-yolk mixture into the egg whites. Pour the batter into the prepared pan, smoothing it evenly to the edges of the pan. Bake for 30 minutes.

While the cake is baking, sift a little confectioners' sugar over a clean tea towel. When the cake is done, remove from the oven (leave the oven on) and turn the warm cake out onto the towel and remove the paper. Roll the cake up, beginning at the narrow end; the cake should be 11 inches long when you are finished. Set aside to cool at room temperature.

Raise the oven temperature to 350°F and line a baking sheet with sides with foil. Spread the pecans in a single layer and bake, stirring once or twice during the baking time to ensure they are evenly toasted, 8 to 10 minutes. The pecans will give off a wonderful aroma, but be sure to watch them carefully, as they burn easily.

Once the cake is cooled, carefully unroll it and spread the whipped cream on the top of it. Re-roll the cake and refrigerate while you make the icing.

Make the Icing: Using a hand mixer or stand mixer on low speed, combine the confectioners' sugar and cocoa powder.

Place the milk in a microwave-safe cup and heat on high for 20 seconds. Add the hot milk and all of the remaining ingredients to the confectioners' sugar mixture and beat on low speed until well blended. Increase the speed to medium-high and beat for 1 minute. Set aside to cool for 20 to 30 minutes.

Ice the cake and cover the top and sides with the toasted pecans. Keep refrigerated until ready to serve.

Aunt Peggy's Apple Pie

Aunt Peggy really wasn't my aunt; she was my mother's first cousin, but she and my mother and aunts were very close. Aunt Peggy was the youngest of thirteen children, and at the height of the Bill Clinton/Monica Lewinsky scandal, one of her sisters-in-law died. The funeral was held in a church that my great-grandparents helped found. It should have been the site of great reverence and solemnity that day.

I sat in the back pew with my cousin, one of Aunt Peggy's sons. His brother had been asked to be a pallbearer, but somehow, he had not been included among the pallbearers. I drove Aunt Mimi up to represent the Beaufort side of the family, and Mimi was asked to sit in the family section, but somehow, I was also not included. So my cousin and I sat in the back pew cracking Bill Clinton/Monica Lewinsky jokes one after the other while we waited for the funeral to start.

While we were on the subject, my cousin shared how upset his mother was about how badly the U. S. House of Representatives was treating President Clinton, including talking about impeachment. According to my cousin, Aunt Peggy said, "I don't know what the big deal is. They just had oral sex . . . they only talked about it!"

I asked my cousin if he had straightened her out about that, to which he replied that he wasn't touching that one with a ten-foot pole. Bless her heart. I hope no one ever told her any different.

Aunt Peggy was known for this wonderful apple pie recipe; she always made them for her church's bazaars.

Makes 6 to 8 servings

½ cup granulated sugar

¼ cup packed light brown sugar

3 tablespoons all-purpose flour

½ teaspoon ground cinnamon

¼ teaspoon freshly grated nutmeg

6 to 8 apples, peeled and thinly sliced

1 (14.1-ounce) box refrigerated pie crust (contains 2 pie pastry sheets) (see note)

8 tablespoons (1 stick) unsalted butter

Vanilla ice cream or whipped cream for serving

Preheat the oven to 425°F. Grease a 9-inch pie pan with butter or baking spray with flour.

Combine the sugars, flour, and spices in a large bowl and mix well. Add the sliced apples to the bowl and toss until the apples are well coated with the sugar mixture.

Unroll 1 sheet of the pie pastry and press it into the prepared pan. Pour the apple mixture into the pan, piling the apple slices toward the middle to ensure they will all fit. Cut the butter into pats and place the pats on top of the apples.

Place the remaining sheet of pie pastry on top of the apples and trim the edges to fit the sides of the pan. Crimp together the top and bottom crusts to seal. Cut several slits in the top crust to allow steam to escape. Bake until the crust is golden brown, 45 to 55 minutes. Remove from the oven and serve warm with the vanilla ice cream or whipped cream.

NOTE: I have also made these pies to freeze using a deep-dish pie shell for the bottom crust and 1 of the packaged refrigerated pie crusts for the top crust. They are easy to make two at a time, since both the pie shells and the pie pastry both come in packages of two.

8

Libations

"Shake, Rattle and Roll"

My friend Johnny McAllister created this drink for me shortly before my fortieth birthday and presented the recipe to me in a silver frame. The inscription reads, "This festive drink was inspired by the legendary Mary Martha Greene and was first prepared on Thanksgiving Day 1999 by John A. McAllister, Jr, President of the Mary Greene Fan Club."

Bourbon has long been the drink of choice in my family. My daddy was a "brown-liquor" man, and Mother and Mimi always drank bourbon (unless they had one of George's Peach Daiquiris [p. 219]). Mother and Mimi were of the generation in which a lady did not fix her own cocktail if a man was present to do so—but Mimi would rattle the ice in her glass to signify when she was ready for another. If a man didn't get up to fix her another drink, she'd rattle it again and look sort of pitifully into the glass, as if to say, "Oh, that ice is so lonely in there with nothing to keep it company." If the hint *still* was not received, the rattling would become increasingly louder until it finally reached a decibel level that could deafen you if you didn't get up and fix that cocktail! All the women in my family that were of that generation rattled their ice when they were ready for another "cheers," as they referred to their cocktails.

Most of these matriarchs were gone by the time the newest generation of the family came along, but one night, one of my cousin's little boys was sitting at my breakfast counter drinking ginger ale. He looked at me when he finished it, and out of nowhere, he rattled the ice in the glass. His dad looked at him and said, "We don't do that at Aunt Mae-Mae's house!"

I replied, "Honey, he can't help it. I swear, it's genetic."

The Mary Greene

While we are all capable of fixing our own cocktails, isn't it nice to sit back every once in a while, rattle the ice in your glass, and have some nice, young gentleman get up and fix it for you?

Makes 1 drink

Crushed ice

1¼ ounces bourbon

½ teaspoon freshly squeezed lime juice

3 dashes cherry or orange bitters

1 maraschino cherry plus 1 teaspoon maraschino cherry syrup

4 ounces (½ cup) diet ginger ale, chilled

Per Johnny's instructions: Begin with a 10-ounce sterling-silver mint julep cup. Half fill the cup with the crushed ice. Combine the bourbon, lime juice, and bitters in the cup and then add the cherry and cherry syrup. Stir with a sterling-silver iced teaspoon. Fill to the top with the diet ginger ale and serve with a linen cocktail napkin.

Garden Party Punch

This punch was served at my parents' wedding in 1953 and at probably every tea and event my mother hosted after that. I remember her making the tea for it in large gallon-size pickle jars placed on the back porch because "sun tea" didn't get "cloudy."

After all the ingredients were combined in her big canning pot, she'd divide it up into large plastic containers and freeze it so she could pull out however much she needed for any particular event. Canned juices can be hard to find these days, so if you can't find them, just substitute 6 cups of each kind of bottled or fresh juice. Fill a Bundt pan with some of the punch and freeze to make an ice ring if you are serving the punch in a punch bowl. This will keep the punch cold, and hopefully ensure you have some of the ice ring left over so that you can make frozen whiskey sours (recipe follows).

Makes 50 (1-cup) servings

- 1 gallon cold water
- 4 family-size tea bags
- 6 cups granulated sugar
- 3 cups room-temperature water
- 2 (7.5-ounce) bottles frozen lemon juice or the freshly squeezed juice of 12 lemons
- 1 (46-ounce) can orange juice
- 1 (46-ounce) can grapefruit juice
- 1 (46-ounce) can pineapple juice
- 2 quarts ginger ale

Pour the cold water over the tea bags into a gallon-size or larger bottle. Set aside to steep for 12 hours. Remove and discard the tea bags.

Combine the sugar and room-temperature water in a saucepan over medium heat and bring to a boil. Boil until the sugar is fully dissolved, making a simple syrup. Remove from the heat and set aside to cool to room temperature.

Combine the tea, simple syrup, and juices in a large stockpot or canning pot and refrigerate or freeze in smaller containers several days before serving.

Just before you are ready to serve, add the ginger ale. Serve.

Frozen Whiskey Sours

I once made Mother's Garden Party Punch for a reception held at the home of a dear friend after the funeral of her devout Methodist mother. I made an ice ring to go in the punch, which was served in a beautiful sterling silver punch bowl that had belonged to the deceased and had been lovingly polished by her daughter the morning of the funeral.

After the reception was over, I fished the partially melted ice ring out of the bowl and placed it in a smaller plastic bowl, along with the rest of the punch. I brought it back to my house, added several cups of bourbon, and poured it in a pitcher that could go in the freezer. The next afternoon, I appeared again at the home of the bereaved, ready to share the sunset and a wonderful frozen whiskey sour with them. It wasn't exactly turning water into wine, but it just might be the Lowcountry version of that miracle!

Makes 8 to 12 drinks

- ½ recipe Garden Party Punch (p. 217)
- 3 to 4 cups bourbon or whisky
- 1 maraschino cherry per drink plus a little maraschino cherry syrup

Combine all the Garden Party Punch and bourbon or whiskey in a freezer-safe container and freeze for at least 12 hours or overnight (the contents will not freeze completely solid).

To serve, scrape the frozen mixture into individual glasses. Garnish each with a maraschino cherry and a little of the cherry syrup.

George's Peach Daiquiris

My brother George took the scenic route through South Carolina's colleges and universities. He was four years older than me, but he graduated from college only one year ahead of me. One of his many stops included a stint at the College of Charleston.

George learned exactly two things at the C of C. First, a little old grandmother in a downtown Charleston laundromat taught him to fold a fitted sheet. Second, one of his roommates, who was a bartender, taught him to make a damn fine peach daiquiri. Both proved to be quite useful skills that he transferred to his baby sister. My family had always "put up" peaches in the summertime, and that skill transferred nicely to peach daiquiri making. Substitute tequila for the rum or vodka, and you have a Peacharita!

Makes 4 drinks

2 large fresh, ripe peaches (freestone preferred)

½ cup room-temperature water

¼ to ½ cup granulated sugar

6 ounces (¾ cup) frozen concentrated lemonade or limeade

6 ounces (¾ cup) vodka, light rum, or tequila

2 to 3 cups ice cubes

Fresh peach slices for garnish

Peel and chop the peaches and place them in a 1-pint plastic container.

Combine the room-temperature water and sugar in a saucepan over medium heat and bring to a boil. Boil until the sugar is fully dissolved, making a simple syrup. Remove from the heat and set aside to cool to room temperature.

Pour the cooled simple syrup over the peaches and place the container in the freezer overnight. (You can use this recipe to "put up" peaches in larger batches; just double or triple the recipe accordingly.)

When you are ready to make the daiquiris, break apart the frozen peaches with a knife and place them in a blender. Add the frozen lemonade and liquor and fill the blender with the ice cubes. Pulse until smooth and fully blended.

Pour the mixture into stemmed wine glasses and serve garnished with the fresh peach slices.

International Velvet

One year for Christmas, I took my mother and aunts to the Grove Park Inn in Asheville, North Carolina. We enjoyed International Velvets while sitting by the huge fireplace in the Grand Hall.

That Christmas, a friend gave me a pitcher with measurements marked on the side—ostensibly for making Bloody Marys. We discovered the pitcher worked remarkably well for making International Velvets, too, so we made a large batch of them—maybe not the best idea ever. They go down so smoothly that they will sneak up on you!

One of my daddy's drinking rules was that you always had to measure your liquor from a jigger. Now, you could fill up the jigger as many times as you wanted to, but you had to pour them from a jigger. The lines on most jiggers indicate 1 to 2 ounces. If you don't have a jigger but want to make this drink, 1 ounce equals 2 tablespoons.

Makes 1 drink

Crushed ice

1 ounce Bailey's Irish Cream

1 ounce amaretto

1 ounce Kahlua liqueur

1 ounce vodka

1 ounce heavy cream or half-and-half (optional)

Fill a glass with the crushed ice and combine all of the ingredients in the glass. If you like your drink a little creamier, add the cream. Stir and enjoy!

Rosemary's Greyhound

I discovered this drink one summer at the Market Place restaurant in Asheville, North Carolina. It's wonderfully refreshing as a summer drink, and it also makes a terrific signature cocktail for a wedding or summertime soiree. The sweetness of the rosemary-flavored simple syrup cuts the tartness of the grapefruit juice. You can make it for a party by the pitcher, using the same 2:4:1 ratio, but be sure to use a glass pitcher so the acid in the grapefruit juice doesn't interact with metal.

Makes 1 drink

Crushed ice

2 ounces (¼ cup) vodka

4 ounces (½ cup) freshly squeezed pink grapefruit juice

1 tablespoon Rosemary Simple Syrup (recipe follows)

Rosemary sprigs for garnish

Fill a double old-fashioned glass with the ice. Pour the vodka over the ice and add the juice and simple syrup. Stir well and serve garnished with the rosemary sprigs.

ROSEMARY SIMPLE SYRUP

1 cup water

1 cup granulated sugar

3 (4- to 5-inch) sprigs rosemary

Rinse and pat dry the rosemary. Set aside on paper towels. Combine the water and sugar in a small saucepan over low heat. Bring the mixture to a boil and allow to cook for about 5 minutes until sugar is dissolved. Remove from the heat and stir until the sugar is completely dissolved, making a simple syrup.

Place the rosemary in a heatproof jar. Pour the simple syrup over the rosemary and allow to steep for 1 hour or longer. Remove the rosemary and keep stored in the refrigerator for cool summer cocktails.

How I Became the Cheese Biscuit Queen

Hopefully, you've read and enjoyed these stories, and by now you realize that Aunt Mimi—Martha Alice Dobson—was the one true queen of all things cheese biscuits. I'd always helped her make them, but my job was to drop them on to the baking sheets, so I'd never really paid much attention to the mixing process. When Aunt Mimi died suddenly and unexpectedly (if you can consider a stroke at the age of eighty-six unexpected), I was afraid her cheese biscuits were gone forever.

Enter our friends Sandy and Rick Somerall, who are our neighbors in Beaufort. Sandy's parents were celebrating their sixty-fifth wedding anniversary, and Sandy tried making cheese biscuits for the occasion using Mimi's recipe. She called Mother in tears because hers turned out hard and not at all light and crispy, like Mimi's. In the background, Mother heard Sandy's retired Marine Corps pilot husband, Lt. Colonel Rick Somerall, say, "But we're going to have a new orange patio for the party, because they're so hard they will make great pavers."

From left to right, Aunt Mary, Aunt Mimi, Mother, and Gran-Gran pictured on the front steps of the Beaufort house. My mother's hair is the biggest I ever remember it being!

I was coming home just about every weekend anyway to take care of Mother and Aunt Mary, so Mother asked if I would get in the kitchen with her and let her "tell me what to do" so we could make some cheese biscuits for the party for Sandy's parents. Well, the combination of my mother, me, and the words "tell me what to do" had all the makings of a big, fat fuss, but we did it. She showed me all the little tricks Mimi used that came so naturally to her she never, ever thought about writing them down in her recipe.

The cheese biscuits were a hit at the party. Everyone said that they were as good as Mimi's (though I can't agree!), and I've been making them ever since. Rarely does a week go by without me making at least one batch. I still deliver them to Mimi's Beaufort friends and neighbors at Christmas, and as our dear across-the-street neighbor says, "It keeps her alive for all of us."

Thus, the title and crown of Cheese Biscuit Queen was passed on to me. I have already made sure the tradition will be inherited by the subsequent generations. When my cousin Patty's grandsons, William and Thomas Lamar, had to make a family recipe for their school projects, they chose to learn how to make cheese biscuits. They will carry on the tradition and keep Aunt Mimi alive for years to come. Maybe they will be the first Cheese Biscuit Kings!

The conclusion of a beautiful poem by Merrit Malloy entitled "Epitaph" reads, "So when all that is left of me is love, give me away." Food keeps those we love alive, and making their recipes once they're gone fills the void left by their absence, as we continue to share them and "give them away." When I am in the kitchen cooking one of these recipes, I'm always comforted by the memories they inspire. Whether I'm serving pork loin and remembering the funny memories of Aunt Mary's ticker-tape greasy 'possum story or making Dessie's peach cobbler and thinking of her letting George sneak in to eat it out of the pan, that food keeps those I love alive. I hope that as you create these dishes and share them with your family and friends, you'll have given them all the love that is left of these folks who are now gone, and that you've created good memories for your family to share with generations to come.

Love a-plenty!
Mary Martha Greene

Acknowledgments

I am grateful to the many, many people who encouraged and helped me to write this book.

First of all, thank you to my wonderful family, for a treasured childhood filled with great food and great memories. I hope I've made you proud.

To the Windham, Duryea, and Key families who long ago made me one of your own, thank you for allowing me to be a part of your family and for letting me share your stories and recipes, as well.

To Jane Windham Key, thanks for being the *best* best friend and chosen sister anyone could ever have.

To Cynthia Stevens Graubart and Debbie Covington, thanks for helping me figure out how to write a cookbook when I had no idea what I was doing.

To my group of volunteer proofers and editors—Cindy Duryea, the Honorable Carolyn Cason Matthews, Dan Cooper, Judy Cannon, Joy Campbell, Sara Fisher, Liz Norris, David Condon, and especially to Kami Kinard, who performed a massive edit to get it ready for submission—thank you for cleaning up all my mistakes with love.

To my Columbia crew—Karen Blackmon, Lynn Stokes Murray, Shannon Bruning, Angelia Smith-Owens, Shirley Mills, Liz Norris, Carol McAlister, Ruth Straight Ellis, Laddie Howard, and many others who encouraged me along the way—thanks for your perseverance.

To my writing crew—Bren McClain, Suzie Parker Devoe, Lynn T. Smith, Kami Kinard and Joe Palmer—thanks for your support through every step and rewrite.

To my Beaufort friends—Kathleen Harvey, Cassandra King, Lynn and Cele Seldon, Marly Russoff, Bonnie Hargrove, Terry Sweeney, Lanier Laney, Nancy Ritter, Ed Duryea, Michael McFee, Joe Devoe, and Sandy and Rick Somerall—thank you for your love, support, and making my culinary mistakes disappear.

To all of the crew at USC Press, and in particular, Aurora Bell, editor extraordinaire; MacKenzie Collier, publicist extraordinaire; and Pat

Callahan, graphic artist extraordinaire, thanks for taking a chance on a first-time writer with lots of stories but no track record.

To Carrie Tippen for her honest assessment of the manuscript and helpful suggestions on ways to improve it.

To Mary Alice Monroe, Casandra King, Virginia Wills, and Nathalie Dupree, thank you for being writing role models and for the wonderful blurbs you wrote.

To my friends who are hurt that I did not include them in this book—be thankful you didn't do anything embarrassing enough to get a mention!

And to all my youth at the Youth Drop-In Center at the Mental Illness Recovery Center, Inc. (MIRCI), thank you for letting me spend my Wednesday afternoons with you and for teaching me as much about life as I try to teach you about cooking.

Index

About the Author

Mary Martha Greene is an award-winning cook. (Okay, so the award was received in the ninth grade for baking napoleons for State Foreign Language Day, but it *was* first place and she *still* has the trophy!) After this stunning victory, she dreamed of a culinary, or at least a creative, career. Her dream of following in the footsteps of a family friend and running the National Chicken Cooking Contest was waylaid by her family court judge father during her freshman year of college. When she came home for Christmas break, he informed her that she'd be reporting for duty as a page at the State House in January. That led to a forty-year career in government relations and politics, including serving on the staff of Governor Richard W. Riley, lobbying, political action, business development, and consulting.

My third birthday in December 1962. I'm clearly not happy that one of my friends removed my pot from the stove!

Mary regrouped and shared her love of cooking, baking, and entertaining to aid her as she made friends and influenced people in the legislative, political, and fundraising arenas. She's also used her skills to help her clients with business development, including running hospitality suites at conferences, sporting events, and a skybox on the eighteenth green for the PGA Heritage Golf Tournament held on Hilton Head Island, South Carolina.

Mary also teaches baking skills to seventeen- to twenty-five-year-old homeless and at-risk youth every week at the Mental Illness Recovery Center, Inc. (MIRCI) Youth Drop-In Center in Columbia, South Carolina. One of her pupils told her one day that she was like a "culinary Mary Poppins," in that she always pops in to bake with them and brings along a large bag from which she pulls all the ingredients and tools necessary to make whatever they are creating that week. Along with teaching them baking skills, she also helps them learn that sometimes the most important thing you can do for someone is to show up when you say you will and to give them your undivided attention.

Mary is a born-and-reared, die-hard Gamecock fan who in fact watches and cares about the game and also understands the importance of preparing a fabulous tailgate. She loves cooking, entertaining, history, "junk-tiquing," and traveling. She was a caregiver to her grandmother, mother, aunts, and other family members for much of her adult life and learned that the best way to get through caregiving is to find the humor in it.

Mary is known as "Aunt Mae-Mae" to about twenty children she loves as her own—none of whom she has birthed, must discipline, or send to college. She excels in spoiling them and returning them to their parents. She currently serves as house staff to her extremely spoiled cat Queenie, who chose Mary by following the smell of barbeque to her kitchen door. She divides her time between Beaufort, South Carolina, and Columbia, the state capital.